Dorothy L. Sayers

The Christ of the Creeds

& Other Broadcast Messages
to the British People
during World War II

ISBN 978-0-9545636-3-9

Published by the Dorothy L. Sayers Society

Rose Cottage, Malthouse Lane, Hurstpierpoint, West Sussex BN6 9JY

smallprint

Gwynfan, Laundry Lane, Leominster, Herefordshire HR6 8JT

Contents

Preface

Dorothy L. Sayers argued for the truth of Christian doctrine as 'a terrific story about God'. She trusted those who in the early centuries of the Christian era had expressed their opinions (dogmas) in creeds. Their authoritative judgements thus became available to us in summary form as matters to be ignored at our own peril. A creed may be compared to a multiplication table – i.e. a formula for dealing with something – in this case, with number. Once we realize that a creed is also a kind of formula, but this time embodying human experience of God, then we are required to examine our most fundamental assumptions about whether we think things really make sense, and whether goodness and purpose can be recognized in that 'making sense'.

So nothing could be more important for Dorothy L. Sayers personally, and for human society, than that Christian doctrine should be both believed and understood, and the selection of her work included in this book expounds her most fundamental convictions under the extreme pressures created by wartime. She brought all her gifts of intellect and imagination as a professional writer to bear on commending how God acts in the world, especially in respect of the Incarnation and what it reveals about God. Her argument is rich in illustration, deploying a range of analogies both to get us to understand dogma, and to persuade us to comprehend our own role in relation to that of God. She writes of the 'intimate' and 'unbreakable' relationship of the material and the non-material manifest uniquely in the Incarnation, but also exhibited in the union of right means, words and intention in particular sacraments. It is important to note, however, that she thinks in broadly sacramental terms, such as the importance of shared prayer with others, lighting a candle in prayer – an example of using the 'stuff' of the universe in worship, and this is integrally connected with her overall vision, which is far from narrowly ecclesiastical. Thus she is blunt and to the point about abuse of self and others, concerned not only with the destructiveness of self-pity, but with many examples of waste and destruction, of enslavement to some forms of government and financial structures, of wilful stupidity, and dishonest and shoddy work, to name a few of her targets.

Dorothy L. Sayers was also robust about how Christians should think of their own suffering whilst doing everything possible to relieve the suffering of others. Some suffering is self-inflicted, she argued, and as for at least some of the rest, an illuminating initial analogy she uses is that drawn from the sheer ordinariness of wash-day, in which a woman deals with the dirt of a household's laundry, both transforming it, and yet in a sense, never done with it – so much of life is somewhat like that, always something of a struggle. In terms of the apparently limitless human capacity for self-defeat, she argues that we have only two options: to crucify God or to be crucified with God, suffering willingly in however small a way, but in joy and hope suffering in, with and for God to play some small part in making good the damage we do to one another. No good news for those who seek security, therefore, but good news for the innocent who are the only ones who have anything to give in this way, if we believe 'the story of God in Jesus'.

Eurocentric, western, and written out of and in response to major social and political crises – Dorothy L. Sayers nevertheless makes it possible for us to recognize the importance of Christian dogma, how we receive it, and how we transmit it.

Ann Loades CBE

Professorial Fellow
St Chad's College
University of Durham

Acknowledgements

This publication would not have been possible without the help of several exceptional people.

Thanks are due above all to the staff of the Marion E. Wade Center at Wheaton College for their help and encouragement. The Clyde S. Kilby research grant enabled me to visit the Wade Center in June 2007 and find several otherwise untraceable documents. Laura Schmidt gave help well beyond the call of duty in seeking out, scanning and copying obscure letters and scripts. Thank you all.

Erin O'Neill of the BBC Written Archives in Caversham gave invaluable help in tracing and copying microfilm texts and correspondence. Thank you.

Clare Williamson (née Welch) and Sir Nicholas Fenn have kindly allowed me to quote from their fathers' memoirs and correspondence. Many thanks.

Various members of the Dorothy L. Sayers Society gave their expertise, advice and support. Particular thanks are due to Barbara Reynolds, Christopher Dean, Jasmine Simeone, Laura Simmons and Christine Fletcher. Thanks too to Adam Schwartz for generously contributing several pieces of helpful background information.

Thanks also to Kathryn Feldman (www.kathrynfeldman.com), who kindly agreed to produce the cover design.

Martin Bray, Rachel Haigh and Richard Birkett all helped with meticulous proofreading and/or deciphering and transcribing handwritten letters and scripts. Many thanks to you all.

SLB

Introduction

Dorothy L. Sayers never intended to be an apologist or an evangelist. Although she had published several religious poems in her youth, in particular her second book of poetry *Catholic Tales & Christian Songs* (1918), up until 1937 she had never felt any particular desire or calling to explain Christian belief.

Writing the Canterbury Festival play, *The Zeal of Thy House*, in 1937 was a turning point for Sayers in many ways. To explain this, we must remember that she was the daughter of an intelligent clergyman and had spent nearly all her life among educated, well-informed people who, for the majority, had received some form of religious education. Although she had become aware at Oxford that many of her contemporaries were not Christians, but "had been brought up in quite a different way of thinking" and were "thoroughly happy",[1] she had previously tended to assume that Christians knew what they believed and that non-Christians knew more or less why they had rejected the Faith. The reactions to her play, both from the actors and from the audience, surprised her. She had not imagined that so many of the English people were so ignorant of or mistaken about the basic Christian message. As she wrote to Father Herbert Kelly:

> It was interesting to discover, as I did, how many people (whether nominal Christians or not) either were Arians, or believed that the Church taught a purely Arian doctrine. However often they had heard or recited the Creeds, it had obviously never sunk into their minds that Christ was supposed to be God in any real sense of the word.[2]

Others too were:

> ... astonished to hear that the Church considered pride to be a sin at all, having always been under the impression that the sins of the flesh were the only sins that counted.[3]

However, she discovered to her surprise that people wanted to listen to her tentative explanations of Christian doctrine, "especially the young men",[4] and,

---

[1] Barbara REYNOLDS (ed.), *The Letters of Dorothy L. Sayers vol.1, 1899-1935: The Making of a Detective Novelist*, Hodder & Stoughton, 1995, p.85.

[2] Barbara REYNOLDS (ed.), *The Letters of Dorothy L. Sayers vol.2, 1937-1943: from novelist to playwright*, The Dorothy L. Sayers Society, 1997, p.43.

[3] ibid., p.68.

[4] ibid., p.49.

as a result, "always seem[ed] to be expounding the Faith in pubs" to interested colleagues and acquaintances.

The London production of *The Zeal of Thy House* in 1938 had more far-reaching consequences. As Sayers told John Wren-Lewis many years later, she "couldn't escape the normal press interviews ... and, as a result of one of them ... wrote the article 'The Greatest Drama ever Staged' ",[5] explaining that the Gospel story was not boring but, on the contrary "the most exciting drama that ever staggered the imagination of man".[6] In fact, it was *The Daily Mail*, one of the main tabloids, which had asked her to contribute an article for Passion Sunday. This accounts for Dorothy's dynamic, racy and, as she called it, "rather bludgeoning style".[7] However, when those who had requested the article actually read it they "were afraid to print it",[8] and so she gave it to *The Sunday Times*, for whom she had been reviewing detective fiction for over two years. The success of this article, which was also published in pamphlet form, and those which followed it, also in *The Sunday Times*,[9] led to Dorothy receiving numerous invitations, mainly from the clergy, to address groups up and down the country on religious themes.

Creed or Chaos?

Once war broke out, Dorothy Sayers found herself to be in even greater demand and was flooded with invitations to write and speak about the Christian faith. One of these invitations was from the Rt Rev. Alfred Edward John Rawlinson, the Bishop of Derby, known to his friends as Jackie. She probably knew him from the Fellowship of St Alban and St Sergius, a group promoting greater understanding between Anglicans and Christians from the Russian Orthodox tradition, with which Dorothy and her friend Charles Williams had had some involvement, and of which Rawlinson was president at this period. She accepted Rawlinson's invitation to speak to The Church Tutorial Classes Association's biennial festival in Derby on May 4 1940.

---

[5] Quoted in David COOMES, *A Careless Rage for Life*, Lion, 1992, p.207.
[6] Dorothy L. SAYERS, "The Greatest Drama Ever Staged", *The Sunday Times*, 3 April, 1938.
[7] Letter to Mr S. Dark, editor of The Church Times, 6 April 1938, in *The Letters of Dorothy L. Sayers vol.2: from novelist to playwright*, p.72.
[8] idem.
[9] eg. "The Triumph of Easter" (17 April 1938), "The Food of the Full-Grown" (9 April 1939) and "What do We Believe?" (10 September 1939).

Dorothy, who always took care to give her books and speeches a memorable title, called her talk *Creed or Chaos?*, following the example of Eric Mascall's *Death or Dogma?*,[10] which she had much admired. It was a great success and sold very well when it was published as a pamphlet by Hodder & Stoughton on June 10. However, even before publication, copies of the text were sent to *The Christian News-Letter* and to the Religious Broadcasting Department of the BBC,[11] which would add another activity to Sayers' already crowded life at the time.

James Welch, an Anglican clergyman in the Evangelical tradition and former missionary in Nigeria, took over from Freddie Iremonger as Director of Religious Broadcasting at the BBC in the summer of 1939. He had heard and much appreciated Sayers' broadcast nativity play for Christmas 1938, *He That Should Come*, and as a result, in February 1940, invited her to write the cycle of plays on the life of Christ which would become *The Man Born to Be King.* His assistant, the Presbyterian Eric Fenn, a member of the influential think-tank the Moot, was also an admirer of Dorothy's. He had been greatly impressed with the Canterbury production of *The Zeal of Thy House* and had requested permission to put on an amateur performance at a Student Christian Movement conference in 1938. When Dorothy was forced to refuse on account of the forthcoming London production, he helped out as much as he could with publicity. Welch and Fenn had great plans for change in religious broadcasting, which were slightly held up by evacuation of the Religious Broadcasting Department to Bristol at the outbreak of war and then, when Bristol was bombed in an attempt to destroy the port, by their second move to Bedford. Until Welch took over, only clergymen had been allowed to preach or give religious talks on the radio, but the new director, in an attempt to "overcome popular prejudice against all things parsonic",[12] persuaded the Archbishop of Canterbury, Cosmo Lang, to allow prominent lay people to do so. Lang, who had been very impressed by some of the lay preachers in the Frank Buchman's Moral Rearmament group, gave his permission. As Welch later wrote to Sayers, as soon as he had read and been excited by her *Creed or Chaos?* address:

---

[10] E. L. MASCALL, *Death or Dogma? – Christian Faith & Social Theory*, SPCK, 1937.

[11] It is most probable, although we have no direct evidence, that Dorothy sent the text to J. H. Oldham at *The Christian News-Letter*, who forwarded it to his close friend and collaborator, Eric Fenn, at the BBC.

[12] Kenneth M. WOLFE, The Churches & the British Broadcasting Corporation 1922-1956, SCM Press, 1984, p.147.

I asked my colleague Eric Fenn to invite you to give two talks in August, and I am very glad you have accepted – don't spare the dynamite![13]

Although Dorothy did accept the invitation, it was with some reluctance. She explained her misgivings to Eric Fenn:

I am increasingly uneasy about these personal appearances in the role of Christian apologist. The plays about the life of Christ are a different matter – that sort of writing is my job. When I use the direct appeal, I am constantly haunted by the feeling that I am running counter to my proper calling.[14]

For this reason she insisted:

… do make it clear that all I propose to do is to explain, to the best of my ability, what the Church thinks about those subjects, and that I am not bringing any "new" lights of my own to bear upon them. I am not a prophet, but only a sort of painstaking explainer of official dogma – [15]

There was also the problem of time. Sayers was extremely busy with several projects, including *The Man Born to Be King* and *The Mind of the Maker*. Less than a month before the first broadcast, she wrote to Fenn, explaining why she hadn't even begun to think about what she was going to say:

I'm trying to finish a book on the Creative Mind, and some tomfool paper wants to know by next Friday 'whether Hitlers have a place in the Divine scheme of things'!![16] I know you wanted something on the lines of "Creed or Chaos?" but your letter is with my agents and I can't remember whether it was the importance of dogma or the nature of sin you wanted me to talk about… I will talk, if you like, about any of the following: the Christ of the Creeds; the Gospel of Sin; the Judgement of God; the Sacrament of Matter.[17]

Fenn chose "The Christ of the Creeds" and "The Sacrament of Matter", giving the overall title *Creed or Chaos?* to the mini-series. They were broadcast on August 11 and August 18 1940.

---

[13] Unpublished letter from J. W. Welch to Dorothy L. Sayers, 10 July 1940, Wade Center, File 433/109.

[14] *The Letters of Dorothy L. Sayers vol.2: from novelist to playwright*, p.165.

[15] ibid., p.171.

[16] Dorothy's article, "Devil, Who Made Thee?" was published in the August 1940 edition of *The World Review*.

[17] ibid., p.170/171.

Although Dorothy had done several broadcasts before, most of these had been informal discussions or interviews. This was her first formal talk on a serious subject and the start was "wavering and uncertain"[18] because the technician, a certain Mr Barnes, kept urging her to slow down. As a result, according to Eric Fenn, "the lower registers of [her] voice came into operation a bit too slowly, so that the opening was a bit difficult to listen to".[19] After about a page, however, she "damned Mr Barnes and took [her] own pace",[20] which seemed to solve the problem. From then on Dorothy and the BBC agreed that she naturally spoke more quickly than most people and she would in future read six pages of typed text in ten minutes.

Despite the technical difficulties, the talk was an overwhelming success. Eric Fenn and his wife both liked it, as did the many people who wrote to the BBC to express their approval. One of these, Isabelle Grey, a member of the Salvation Army, wrote to Sayers: "I listened to your address on the wireless and I felt wonderfully strengthened. You seemed so sure of what you were saying".[21] More importantly, the press was also favourable. W. E. Williams, one of the regular columnists in *The Listener*, wrote:

> In the way of accomplished exposition I have seldom heard anything more admirable than Dorothy L. Sayers on the essentials of Christian belief (August 11). She tackled a most recalcitrant theological topic without making any concessions to mere piety. In one of his moods of elephantine obstinacy Dr Johnson once ridiculed the notion of a woman in the pulpit. I'd back Dorothy Sayers to put the case for Christianity better than many of our wireless padres; and if she will promise to abate a wayward high note in her voice, I will gladly listen to her for a month of Sundays.[22]

The second talk, "The Sacrament of Matter", went without a hitch. Dorothy was particularly delighted that she had "succeeded in satisfying the *Church Times*"[23] as she had been afraid she "might get trounced for making the basis

[18] Unpublished letter from Dorothy L. Sayers to Eric Fenn, 14 August 1940, Wade Center, File 444/7b.
[19] Unpublished letter from Eric Fenn to Dorothy L. Sayers, 12 August 1940, Wade Center, File 444/8.
[20] Unpublished letter from Dorothy L. Sayers to Eric Fenn, 14 August 1940, Wade Center, File 444/7b.
[21] Unpublished letter, 17 September 1940, in private ownership.
[22] W. E. WILLIAMS, "The Spoken Word", *The Listener*, 15 August 1940, p.248.
[23] *The Letters of Dorothy L. Sayers vol.2: from novelist to playwright*, p.174.

of the sacramental position too broad".[24] There was a certain relief as well that no teetotallers had "written to protest at the sacramental drinking of healths".[25] Dorothy was also pleased to get a letter from the future Cardinal Heenan telling her "how many people like the talks"[26] and sent him a copy of both the scripts. Welch and Fenn at the Religious Broadcasting Department were more than satisfied and wrote to tell Dorothy so. Fenn felt particularly that she had "got home in the last paragraph to great effect",[27] while James Welch admitted: "I am rather hard-boiled, but your last talk really did get under my skin".[28]

To start with, everyone concerned expected *The Listener* to publish the talks. When it became apparent that this was not going to happen, a number of people, including one pensioner of 81, wrote to Dorothy "complaining that the talks were not published in the *Listener* and asking whether they [were] going to appear in pamphlet form".[29] Her standard reply right through the autumn was that they were going to be published. Yet they were not. The reason for this is unknown, but may well have been connected with the severe shortage of paper at that stage of the war.

Dorothy's willingness to do these talks in the first place and her desire to have them published were based on her firm conviction, which she had already expressed at Derby, that "it is fatal to imagine that everybody knows quite well what Christianity is and needs only a little encouragement to practise it."[30] On the contrary, by this time she was prepared to affirm that:

> Not one person in a hundred has the faintest idea what the Church teaches about God, or Man or society or the person of Jesus Christ. If you think I am exaggerating, ask the Army chaplains.[31]

She attributed this problem, at least in part, to the language used by the clergy to express Christian doctrine, which she described as "a set of technical theological terms which nobody has taken the trouble to translate into language

---

[24] idem.

[25] ibid., p.179.

[26] ibid., p.180.

[27] Unpublished letter from Eric Fenn to Dorothy L. Sayers, 19 August 1940, Wade Center, File 444/6.

[28] Unpublished letter from James Welch to Dorothy L. Sayers, 24 August 1940, Wade Center, File 433/104.

[29] *The Letters of Dorothy L. Sayers vol.2: from novelist to playwright*, p.174.

[30] "Creed or Chaos?", *Creed or Chaos?*, Sophia Institute Press, 1995, p.31.

[31] idem.

relevant to everyday life".[32] This, however, was not entirely the fault of the clergy, but a result of the inadequate training they had received. As she explained to John Heenan: "So few parsons are really trained in the use of words. They use the standard technical phrases without quite realising how they sound to the ordinary reader or listener."[33] She therefore perceived her role as that of a translator who could come along and say:

> Look here! This isn't just verbiage or mumbo-jumbo. It means something quite concrete and relevant. It applies in the most matter-of-fact way to my everyday experience. In current speech it means this ...[34]

The wide and varied BBC audience also meant that Dorothy tried to make her talks completely free of "sectarian skewers"[35] and "acceptable to all sorts, from Catholics to Quakers".[36]

But why talk about the Creeds? John Thurmer has already pointed out that all her life Sayers "had believed and been fascinated by the Christian creeds".[37] She also considered that these statements of faith, shared by all the mainstream denominations, were extremely important. Several years after these broadcasts, she explained her reasons to a Quaker schoolgirl:

> The formulation of a Creed is desirable in order that the Church may understand her own mind and put her opinion on record. Otherwise she may find that what people are teaching in her name is no longer Christianity, but has insensibly turned into something quite different. If you study the history of the Creeds, you will find that their clauses are all directed to safeguarding the Faith against some perversion which was creeping in – nearly always due, originally, to over-emphasis upon some point which was sound enough if kept in its proper place.[38]

Therefore, from Sayers' point of view, by sticking to the Creeds, she could be sure that she was presenting the faith of the universal Church and not some

---

[32] ibid., p.37.

[33] *The Letters of Dorothy L. Sayers vol.2: from novelist to playwright*, p.179/180.

[34] Unpublished letter to Dom Ralph Russell, 28 October 1941, Wade Center File 406/71.

[35] *The Letters of Dorothy L. Sayers vol.2: from novelist to playwright*, p.329.

[36] ibid., p.179.

[37] John THURMER, *Reluctant Evangelist: Papers on the Christian Thought of Dorothy L. Sayers*, The Dorothy L. Sayers Society, 1996, p.38.

[38] Barbara REYNOLDS (ed.), *The Letters of Dorothy L. Sayers vol.4, 1951-1957: In the Midst of Life*, The Dorothy L. Sayers Society, 2000, p.3.

idea of her own. The Creeds, as she stated in her preface to *The Mind of the Maker*, are, from the Church's point of view, "not expressions of opinion but statements of fact",[39] objective declarations "about the nature of God and the universe".[40] Moreover, if the first talk, "The Christ of the Creeds", provided as a clear an explanation as she could produce of Christian dogma, the second, concentrating on the sacramental approach to life, was intended to show the implications of this dogma for the believer. Sayers shared with Charles Williams and many other Anglo-Catholic writers of the time a theology centred on the Incarnation, and found in this central truth the justification for her religious practice and indeed her whole way of understanding the world we live in. As she explained to the Chelmsford Arts Association in 1952:

> From the Incarnation springs the whole doctrine of sacraments – the indwelling of the mortal by the immortal, of the material by the spiritual, the phenomenal by the real. After an analogous manner, we all bear about with us not only the immortal soul but also the glorified body in which we shall be known at the Resurrection, though now it is known only to God, or to those to whom love may reveal it.[41]

The strength of this position, as Dorothy's second talk reveals, is that it provides the basis of an ethical system applicable to industrial relations, the environment, political power, art, architecture, and business practice, as well as personal relationships. It also connects belief and behaviour, with each supporting the other in a coherent world view. For this reason, church leaders and ordinary people of all backgrounds were delighted with Dorothy's talks and the Religious Broadcasting Department of the BBC were determined to use her talents again.

The Religions Behind the Nation

In December 1939, Pope Pius XII included in his Christmas message a five-point plan for peace in Europe, which clearly indicated his opposition to the ideology and activities of the Nazi regime. The same month, Dorothy L.

---

[39] *The Mind of the Maker*, Mowbray, 1994, p.xvii.
[40] idem.
[41] "The Poetry of the Image in Dante & Charles Williams", *Further Papers on Dante*, Methuen, 1957, p.187.

Sayers finished writing a message to the British nation, entitled *Begin Here*, which was, at the same time, a study of those factors in the history of Europe which had led to the Second World War, "a consideration of peace terms"[42] and, in Sayers' own words, a suggestion to her readers of "some creative line of action along which they, as individuals, can think and work towards the restoration of Europe".[43]

The Pope's message, somewhat obviously, had the wider repercussions and, in Britain, led to a joint declaration, or manifesto, a year later, signed by the Archbishop of Canterbury (Cosmo Gordon Lang), the Archbishop of York (William Temple), the Cardinal Archbishop of Westminster (Arthur Hinsley) and the Moderator of the Free Church Federal Council (Walter H. Armstrong). This manifesto, published in *The Times* on December 21 1940, showed an unprecedented level of cooperation between the leaders of the principal Christian denominations in Britain. Apart from the united front presented by the signatories, it was also of interest on account of the five extra points which the British church leaders had added to the Pope's original five, indicating the standards by which any economic situations and proposals could be tested:

- Extreme inequality in wealth or possessions should be abolished;
- Every child, regardless of race or class, should have equal opportunities of education, suitable for the development of his peculiar capacities;
- The family as a social unit must be safeguarded;
- The sense of a Divine vocation must be restored to man's daily work;
- The resources of the earth should be used as God's gifts to the whole human race, and used with due consideration for the needs of the present and future generations.

This joint declaration gave rise to considerable interest and comment in the press and on the radio. It was not, however, the only initiative by Christian leaders at the time to attract attention. The Malvern Conference, organised by William Temple, on the theme of "The Life of the Church & the Order of Society", originally planned for October 1940, finally took place at the beginning of January 1941, just a couple of weeks after the joint declaration. Dorothy Sayers had been invited to participate as a result of *Begin Here*, which had greatly impressed Temple, and spoke for forty-five minutes on "The Church's

---

[42] From the dust jacket of the second impression of *Begin Here* (Gollancz, February 1940).
[43] *Begin Here*, p.5.

Responsibility".[44] This was probably Sayers' most profound and complex work of applied theology. It clearly demonstrates both the strength of her belief in the radical and dynamic nature of the Gospel message and her conviction that the Church is called to play an uncompromising, prophetic role in this sinful world. If, as Freddie Iremonger believed to be the case for all the talks, "only a small minority of the listeners understood even what the issues were in the sociological and theological fields",[45] some of those present, including Eric Fenn, were very impressed.

Shortly after Malvern, in an attempt to keep the issues raised by the Archbishop's conference and the joint declaration before the public, Eric Fenn wrote to several well-known Christian speakers, including Dorothy Sayers, asking them to take part in a series originally called "Foundations of Peace", but changed to "The Church Looks Ahead" after pressure from the authorities.[46] It was loosely based on the Church leaders' Ten Points. This series would be broadcast during February and March. During the first week of March, James Welch would also be using the daily "Lift up your Hearts" meditations to discuss the same themes. Most of the speakers, who included Philip Mairet,[47] Professor Hodges,[48] J. H. Oldham,[49] T. S. Eliot and Father D'Arcy, were known to be intellectual heavyweights and many were also, like Fenn, members of the Moot.

Although she would later refer to her talk in this series, "The Religions Behind the Nations",[50] as "a bit of religious twaddle on the air",[51] at the start Dorothy took it very seriously, sending a synopsis to Fenn well in advance and getting Patrick McLaughlin, the vicar of St Thomas, Regent Street, to edit her talk.[52] Eric Fenn "sent [her] outline to Eliot for his delectation before sending

---

[44] Published in *Malvern, 1941*, Longmans, Green & Co., 1941, p.57-78.
[45] F. A. IREMONGER, *William Temple: Archbishop of Canterbury*, Oxford University Press, 1948, p.430.
[46] See Kenneth M. WOLFE, *The Churches & the British Broadcasting Corporation 1922-1956: The Politics of Broadcast Religion*, SCM Press, 1984, p.195.
[47] Editor of *The New English Weekly*.
[48] H. A. Hodges, Professor of Philosophy at Reading University, a specialist in 19th century German philosophy.
[49] Among his many other activities, Oldham was at this time editor of *The Christian News-Letter*.
[50] Published by T. S. Eliot in *The Church Looks Ahead*, Faber & Faber, 1941, p.67-78.
[51] *The Letters of Dorothy L. Sayers vol.2: from novelist to playwright*, p.235.
[52] See Wade Center File 442.

it anywhere else".[53] In this talk, she developed further the theories she had begun to elaborate in *Begin Here* and, basing her analysis on the writings of the Catholic thinker Christopher Dawson,[54] discussed the relationship between religion and culture in Britain at the time.

Sayers took as her starting point Dawson's theory that:

It is the religious impulse which supplies the cohesive force which unifies a society and a culture. The great civilisations of the world do not produce the great religions as a kind of cultural by-product; in a very real sense the great religions are the foundations on which the great civilisations rest.[55]

Dawson went on to conclude that "a society which has lost its religion becomes sooner or later a society which has lost its culture".[56] Sayers took this point even further and affirmed that, in the dechristianised European society of her day "ideals such as justice, equality and freedom [were] left without rational and doctrinal basis", with the result that, "in the absence of any alternative guide, money becomes the ruling power".[57] She did not find the talk easy to write, mainly on account of the limited time available for such a complex subject. She wrote an explanatory note to Eric Fenn:

A major difficulty is that I must mention the difference made to man's confidence in his convictions by Incarnation doctrine, but there is no space to explain why it was that the Incarnation made all this difference.[58]

Although the Religious Broadcasting Department was very pleased with the series, Dorothy had mixed feelings about reactions to her own contribution. Her image of the beads and the string, in particular, had been well-received, but, as she ruefully pointed out to Eric Fenn, the talk seemed to have "produced a more than usually fruity crop of candidates for the loony bin"[59] in her correspondence.

---

[53] Unpublished letter from Eric Fenn to Dorothy L. Sayers, 14 February 1941, BBC Written Archives, File 910 2A.
[54] Sayers knew Dawson personally and he had sent her a review copy of *Beyond Politics* in 1939. She referred to it in *Begin Here* and included it in the reading list at the end of the book.
[55] Christopher DAWSON, *Progress & Religion*, Sheed & Ward, 1938, p.245 (First published in 1929).
[56] idem.
[57] See synopsis of talks, Wade Center File 442/19.
[58] Unpublished letter from Dorothy L. Sayers to Eric Fenn, 5 February 1941, BBC Written Archives, File 910 2A.
[59] *The Letters of Dorothy L. Sayers vol.2: from novelist to playwright*, p.242.

God the Son

In her initial reply to Eric Fenn's invitation to participate in the *Church Looks Ahead* series, Dorothy passed on a criticism from a listener to a friend of hers that "the brand of religion emanating from the BBC is much more theist than Christian",[60] that "God the Father is presented too much in the aspect of a divine dictator managing things from above"[61] and that, as a result, people were left with the impression that...

> ... there is somebody called God and a subsequent, inferior, but more sympathetic person called the Son of God, who had nothing to do with creating the world, and whose part in running it is rather that of a foreman of the works sadly put upon by the management.[62]

The Religious Broadcasting Department's response to this was to organise a major series on the Nicene Creed for the Forces wavelength and, as part of it, asked Dorothy to do six talks on the clauses referring to Jesus Christ. She accepted, insisting on the title "God the Son", in order to avoid the confusion often associated with the term Son of God which, as she later explained to D. G. Jarvis, "tends to suggest that the second person of the Trinity begins and ends with the human Jesus".[63]

This series of weekly broadcasts on the Creed, which ran from April 20 to September 28 1940, was one of Eric Fenn's biggest projects for the BBC and involved an interesting array of well-known speakers representing all the main denominations. A preparatory meeting was arranged to instruct the speakers of the basic issues at stake and the procedure to follow. Dorothy was excused from attending it, possibly because it was felt she was already in the know about all the essentials or possibly because Fenn found her "quite impossible to produce", "not a person very susceptible to advice about this or, I imagine, anything else!".[64] Therefore, the best solution was always "just ... to let her rip and hope".[65] He added, however, on the same occasion, that they "always got on well".[66]

---

[60] ibid., p.232.
[61] idem.
[62] ibid., p.233.
[63] *The Letters of Dorothy L. Sayers vol.2: from novelist to playwright*, p.185.
[64] Eric FENN, Unpublished memoir, p.135/136 (in the possession of Sir Nicholas Fenn).
[65] Idem.
[66] Idem.

Bishop Neville Talbot[67] was asked to do four introductory talks, which he entitled "Questions Men Ask". The Rev. John Williams, working as Fenn's assistant on the project, told Sayers that "the particular bee buzzing in [Talbot's] bonnet is the idea that credal statements are cold and clammy unless you first get fired by the red-hot experiences and agonising questions which they are the answer to".[68] Less than completely convinced, Sayers told Eric Fenn:

> I expect he will cope only too earnestly with the question about why the Church believes. After the sort of opening he will produce, it may be a good thing to have a sober statement of what she actually *does* believe![69]

Fenn sympathised, saying that Talbot was "quite unaccountable",[70] and telling Dorothy that when he had once taken Talbot to Berlin, they had "nearly landed in a concentration camp!"[71]

Talbot was followed by the Jesuit Father John Murray,[72] who had already done a lot of work for the Religious Broadcasting Department and whom Dorothy knew from her involvement with the Sword of the Spirit.[73] Murray was asked to speak about God the Father and produced a mini-series of three talks, under the general title "First Things First". Sayers was pleased with this choice of speaker

---

[67] Neville Talbot, who was living in Nottingham at the time, was the former Bishop of Pretoria (1920-1939). He came from a well-known Anglican family, his father having been Bishop of Winchester. Neville was a very successful army chaplain during the First World War, working alongside the Rev. Tubby Clayton, the founder of Toc H. Talbot House, the headquarters of Toc H, was named after Neville's younger brother Gilbert, killed in action in July 1915. Neville worked a lot with the Royal Air Force chaplains during the Second World War. Dorothy Sayers knew him personally and, in 1939, had accepted an invitation from him to speak first to the clergy and then to the young people in Nottingham (see *The Letters of Dorothy L. Sayers vol.2: from novelist to playwright*, p.116-118).

[68] *The Letters of Dorothy L. Sayers vol.2: from novelist to playwright*, p.244.

[69] idem.

[70] Unpublished letter from Eric Fenn to Dorothy L. Sayers, 1 April 1941, Wade Center File 443.

[71] idem.

[72] Murray was at the time editor of *The Month*. He was known for the importance he attributed to the concept of natural law and for his willingness to participate in oecumenical projects. He was the first Roman Catholic to support Sayers' and Welch's project for an "Oecumenical Penguin" or common statement of the Highest Common Factor of Christian belief. He was also a member of the CRAC (Central Religious Advisory Committee of the BBC) at the time.

[73] Movement founded in 1940 by Cardinal Hinsley which "sought to institutionally unite all people of good will against the totalitarian threat to traditional Western ideals". (Adam SCHWARTZ, "Swords of Honor: The Revival of Orthodox Christianity on Twentieth-Century Britain", *Logos 4:1*, Winter 2001, p.11-33).

and wrote to Fenn that Murray, "being a Jesuit ... will probably give a proper dogmatic basis from which to work, and erect the scaffolding for the Trinitarian formula. All the better."[74] After Dorothy's own six talks came Professor H. G. Wood[75] with four sessions on the Holy Spirit and Dom Bernard Clements O.S.B.[76] with three talks on the Church. Professor R. D. Whitehorn[77] had four weeks to finish the series off with baptism, forgiveness, death/resurrection and eternal life.

Sayers took a whole month to respond to Eric Fenn's initial invitation to take part in the series on the Creed, finally replying on March 20 1941 that she was "sorry to have kept God the Son waiting all this time"[78] and enclosing a rough outline of what she wanted to say. Six days later she sent Fenn a draft of her first two talks. Her main problem came from the fact that the talks were to be just ten minutes long while "the Creed itself is packed as much as an egg with meat".[79] As a result, she found it was "rather difficult to unpack it, when you have to try and explain everything in everyday language".[80] Another difficulty came from not knowing what the speakers before her in the series were going to say. In the same envelope as the draft scripts of her talks, she asked Fenn whether John Murray was "going to be so obliging as to deal at all with the Trinitarian formula",[81] hoping very hard that he was. She also wrote to Neville Talbot to find out if he was intending to give any "preliminary instruction on the nature of man and the nature of sin", as, in her opinion, modern man found "the whole concept of sin ... unfamiliar and unconvincing", but she would not have the time to "squeeze [it] into a ten-minute talk"[82] on the Incarnation.

Eric Fenn's reply was encouraging. He sent her a 7-page, 1500-word epistle with detailed comments on the texts. He liked her scripts very much and particularly appreciated her way of dividing up the series – two talks on

---

[74] *The Letters of Dorothy L. Sayers vol.2: from novelist to playwright*, p.245.
[75] H. G. Wood was a Quaker working as both Professor of Theology at Birmingham University and Director of Studies at Woodbrook Quaker Study Centre.
[76] Vicar of the very Anglo-Catholic All Saints, Margaret Street, just down the road from Broadcasting House in London. He was one of the most popular radio preachers with the Forces (see WOLFE, *The Churches & the British Broadcasting Corporation 1922-1956: The Politics of Broadcast Religion*, p.272).
[77] A Free Churchman and well-known historian of Nonconformity in Britain.
[78] *The Letters of Dorothy L. Sayers vol.2: from novelist to playwright*, p.242.
[79] ibid., p.243.
[80] idem.
[81] idem.
[82] Unpublished letter from Dorothy L. Sayers to Neville Talbot, 12 May 1941, Wade Center File 447/32.

"Lord", two on "Jesus" and two on "Christ". He also considered that what she had to say would "leave … a clear picture of what the Church believes and ought to teach".[83] Sayers acted on nearly all his suggestions and was especially enthusiastic about his statement "people fought about this word" with reference to the controversial term *homoiousion* (of one substance), which defeated the Arians at Nicaea.[84] On the other hand, she did not let herself be swayed by Fenn's desire that she begin straight off with a question. She wrote "children's hour stuff!" in the margin of his letter and insisted:

> I'm *not good* at the direct personal appeal … It always makes me embarrassed, and I can feel my voice getting that awful, wheedling, children's hour intonation – very bright and encouraging, like somebody trying to screw answers out of an idiot school. Flat statement and argument is my natural line, and I shall make a ghastly mess of the other if I try it.[85]

Her reply from Neville Talbot was much less satisfactory. He was not finding it easy to write his "four addresses of hideous brevity". His priority, he explained, had been "to take hearers down … to the historical bone" and, in doing so had "left doctrine out"[86] completely and had "only rather incidentally … referred to sin".[87] His sole attempt to help Dorothy had been to leave "a hook or link" at the end of his fourth talk "onto which doctrine can be hung".[88] The hook in question was the following paragraph:

> Do you detect in these last words of mine that I refer to the essence of the Church's creed, the truth of the Incarnation? In tracing the road to Calvary I said nothing about it. Why? Because it was in nobody's mind right up to the Cross. The disciples of Jesus were Jews to the end. Before His death they got no further than the hope that He was the Christ of God, the Messiah. But the Gospel of God is the Cross, to which I have pointed you, carried into the revelation of His Divine Sonship.[89]

---

[83] Unpublished letter from Eric Fenn to Dorothy L. Sayers, 1 April 1941, Wade Center File 443.

[84] See *The Letters of Dorothy L. Sayers vol.2: from novelist to playwright*, p.245.

[85] *The Letters of Dorothy L. Sayers vol.2: from novelist to playwright*, p.245.

[86] Unpublished letter from Bishop Neville Talbot to Dorothy L. Sayers, 7 May 1941, Wade Center File 447/34.

[87] Unpublished letter from Bishop Neville Talbot to Dorothy L. Sayers, 16 May 1941, Wade Center File 447/30.

[88] idem.

[89] Wade Center File 447/31-32.

Dorothy was incandescent and, in her own words, "reduced to complete pulp"[90] by this information. She expressed her frustration somewhat forcibly to John Williams, exclaiming:

> ... in FOUR talks devoted to *Why* we want a God to believe in, it has not occurred to him to explain what is meant by the word "Sin"!!!! You wouldn't think anybody *could* overlook that theological trifle, would you?[91]

This meant that she now had to "squash Sin into two minutes filched from the Incarnation".[92] Another exclamation in the same letter, declaring that she had "ceased to put [her] trust in Jesuits or in any child of man"[93] leads us to believe that Father John Murray had not come up to scratch on the Trinity either!

Considering the many other things she was doing at the time, Dorothy had to write these talks in a hurry. Eric Fenn's editing was essential. The original draft to the fifth talk, for instance, is considerably longer and less elegant than the final version. She even made the occasional mistake. Fenn was, for example, obliged to point out: "...you refer to Bethlehem as in Galilee. Bethlehem, of course, was in Judaea".[94] Dorothy was grateful for this help, claiming that the error was "a pure slip".[95] Writing the talks was indeed a very difficult task, requiring an extremely compact style. For the third one, as she explained to John Williams, even when she had managed to divert miracles and the Holy Ghost, there was still "'came down from heaven', 'incarnate' and the doctrine of perfect Manhood" to explain, which seemed "to present stiff enough problems for a ten minute talk".[96]

Dorothy broadcast the first two "God the Son" talks live and stayed to record the others on 15 June – taking taxis to and from Witham at the BBC's expense. She insisted on very short introductions, but warned the announcer for the fifth talk: "... let him not say: 'The World's Desire – Miss Sayers',

---

[90] *The Letters of Dorothy L. Sayers vol.2: from novelist to playwright*, p.260.
[91] idem.
[92] idem.
[93] idem. Allusion to the biblical verse from Psalm 146: "O put not your trust in princes, nor in any child of man: for there is no help in them."
[94] Unpublished letter from Eric Fenn to Dorothy L. Sayers, 9 June 1941, Wade Center File 443/8.
[95] Unpublished letter from Dorothy L. Sayers to Eric Fenn, 10 June 1941, Wade Center File 443/7.
[96] Unpublished letter from Dorothy L. Sayers to the Rev. J.G. Williams, 12 May 1941, Wade Center File 443/18.

which would be indelicate as well as untrue".[97] John Williams, who had not worked with her before was delighted and thought the talks had "been going across admirably". He was particularly impressed by "the ease with which you get through so much in such a short space of time".[98] He also gleefully remarked that: "They were probably pretty stiff going for many listeners, but no doubt that served to increase their respect for the Church's intelligence".[99] Dorothy replied that she had enjoyed doing the talks and that she agreed "they were rather stiff going for the majority".[100] However, from her point of view, this was not a bad thing.

In spite of any possible intellectual difficulties for the listeners, reactions to the "God the Son" series were generally positive. In addition to the "usual collection of tracts and lunatics"[101] and two protests about her treatment of the Resurrection, "one accusing [her] of gross materialism and the other of being a Christian Scientist", Dorothy's post contained "a number of thoughtful and appreciative letters asking whether [the] talks were going to be printed",[102] as many people wished to study them in detail. She had her doubts, however, about whether this would be possible, wondering if the whole series "would really make a coherent exposition of the Creed if they were all published together", partly at least because her own contributions were "a good deal more rigid and dogmatic than any of the others".[103] Her misgivings were justified. Hugh Martin of SCM Press, after careful consideration, decided he could not publish the talks as "he felt the book would not make a very satisfactory unity".[104] As a result, they were never published.

Dorothy L. Sayers: Broadcasting Consultant

By September 1940, Dorothy had already agreed to write the series of plays on the life of Christ, *The Man Born To Be King*, for the Religious Broadcasting

---

[97] *The Letters of Dorothy L. Sayers vol.2: from novelist to playwright*, p.260.
[98] Unpublished letter from Rev. J. G. Williams to Dorothy L. Sayers, 16 June 1941, Wade Center, File 443/5.
[99] Unpublished letter from Rev. J. G. Williams to Dorothy L. Sayers, 16 June 1941, Wade Center, File 443/3.
[100] *The Letters of Dorothy L. Sayers vol.2: from novelist to playwright*, p.278.
[101] ibid., p.278-279.
[102] ibid., p.279.
[103] idem.
[104] Unpublished letter from Rev. J. G. Williams to Dorothy L. Sayers, 22 August 1941, Wade Center, File 445/21.

Department of the BBC. In that context, she had started a correspondence with James Welch that would continue, on and off, for the rest of her life. Impressed by her grasp of the challenges and difficulties of religious broadcasting in wartime, Welch invited Dorothy to come to the Langham Hotel in London "to a meeting of the group to discuss ... the spiritual issues of the war".[105] This was the start of Dorothy's work as a consultant on religious broadcasting. We have several accounts of the meeting. Robin Whitworth remembers James Welch, "three regional controllers and four bright young men of Christian motivation ... plus Dorothy Sayers"[106] getting together to discuss the future of religious broadcasting in wartime. He particularly noted a remark of Dorothy's: "There is no doubt that if Christ was now a member of the staff of the BBC, he would be sacked."[107] Dorothy herself thought that she "was there rather in the capacity of *advocatus diaboli*"[108] and found the discussions "a bit depressing".[109]

This meeting was, however, the start of a fruitful correspondence and collaboration between Dorothy and Canon F. A. Cockin of St Paul's Cathedral, who informed her that he had written to James Welch straight after the meeting "to say that the only person whose views I found at all congenial was yourself".[110] She returned the compliment, writing: "I take to you, as the children say, immediately".[111] This led to several meetings with the Canon, another meeting with the committee at Canon Cockin's house on October 8th, participation in an advisory group, and a lot of meticulous work correcting Canon Cockin's draft sermons. For example, the Canon's first attempt at a series of broadcast sermons was ten pages long.[112] Dorothy typed seven pages of corrections and suggestions.[113] She also commented on his second and third drafts before James Welch finally approved the text for broadcasting in November.

---

[105] Unpublished letter from James Welch to Dorothy L. Sayers, 4 September 1940, Wade Center, File 433/99.

[106] Unpublished letter from Robin Whitworth to John Phillips, 30 October 1985, Phillips Papers (PHP 4/1), Henry Martyn Centre, Cambridge.

[107] idem.

[108] Devil's advocate.

[109] Unpublished letter from Dorothy L. Sayers to Canon Cockin, 23 September 1940, Wade Center, File 223/30.

[110] Unpublished letter from Canon F. A. Cockin to Dorothy L. Sayers, 25 September 1940, Wade Center, File 223/27.

[111] Unpublished letter from Dorothy L. Sayers to Canon Cockin, 27 September 1940, Wade Center, File 223/25.

[112] Wade Center, File 469.

[113] Wade Center, File 223/7-13.

Welch was so pleased with Dorothy's help on this project that, immediately afterwards, he involved her in a broadcast mission entitled "Facing 1941" for the first week of the new year. Sending the draft scripts, he asked her to comment on:

> Is the "message" right? What has been omitted that should have been included? Will it appeal to all or to many of our listeners? Is the suggested order and presentation good? What kind of "surround" would you suggest for the various talks?[114]

Once again, Dorothy sent back seven typed pages of in-depth literary, social and theological analysis, suggesting useful quotations from classical and contemporary authors and comparing the drafts with other broadcasts she had heard. She also included a warning that Thursday's script contained a statement on the Incarnation which was "a little Arian in form"[115] and offered some lines of her own verse to correct the imbalance:

> Yet this [sorrow etc.] is nothing if only God will not be indifferent,
> If He is beside me, bearing the weight of His own creation,
> If I may hear His voice among the voices of the vanquished,
> If I may feel His hand touch mine in the darkness,
> If I may look into the hidden face of God
> And read in the eyes of God
> That He is acquainted with grief.[116]

This meticulous, unpaid editing was invaluable to Welch and his colleagues and they often solicited her help. In this way she contributed to many of the Religious Broadcasting Department's most notable successes. For example, she corrected and improved the texts of a much appreciated series of four programmes entitled *Three Men & a Parson*, a kind of religious *Any Questions?*, broadcast in Lent 1941, where three men from different walks of life put before Canon Cockin "some of the questions which many listeners would like to ask a representative of the Church".[117]

---

[114] Unpublished letter from James Welch to Dorothy L. Sayers, 2 November 1940, Wade Center File 469/3.

[115] Wade Center File 223/7-13.

[116] idem. – Sayers originally wrote these lines for her broadcast Nativity play *He That Should Come*. They were cut by Val Gielgud, who thought them dull, but included in the published version.

[117] Dr J. W. WELCH, "Three Men and a Parson", *The Listener*, 21 February 1941, p.3.

By 1943, Dorothy Sayers was no longer writing religious talks or plays for broadcasting herself.[118] However, this was the year when her role as a consultant on religious broadcasting was most fruitful. The letters included in this volume had a tremendous impact on religious broadcasting policy and, more specifically, were the inspiration for the BBC's unofficial mission to the nation during the first quarter of 1944.

This part of the story begins on 10 February 1943, when Ronald Selby Wright, the Radio Padre, gave a live talk to the Armed Forces on faith in God. According to Dorothy's account the next day, after the talk, Selby Wright was asked "whether it was necessary to believe the Creeds and all that".[119] In reply, "he waved the Creeds aside, said it wasn't necessary to remain in the shallows worrying about details – one should go for the deep things and have faith in God".[120] Dorothy added with deep sarcasm:

> Since nobody, up to that point, had mentioned Christ at all, I could only conclude that He was one of the superfluous details to be swept up with the rest of the rubbish, and was really quite surprised to hear Him mentioned afterwards in a parenthesis.[121]

Dorothy was, in fact, livid, stating later that if she could have hit the padre with a brick, she would have thrown it.

The following morning, Dorothy had to write to the BBC to refuse Eric Fenn's invitation to take part in a series of dialogues on *God is Agape*. Before getting down to it, she read the latest copy of *The Christian News-Letter*, edited by Fenn's friend and former boss J. H. Oldham, which included a Mass-Observation report on religion in Britain. She found it profoundly depressing. This was because "judging by the report, nobody would suppose ... that the 'religion' in question was Christianity".[122] In fact, like in the Radio Padre's religious broadcast, Jesus Christ hardly came into the report at all. Her first instinct was to write to *The Christian News-Letter*, but in the end decided to pour out her feelings to James Welch because, as she said: "I can express myself more pungently to you",[123] which she did at considerable length and with great

---

[118] She would do a few more religious talks in 1951 and 1952, but no more specifically dogmatic or apologetic addresses.
[119] "Christ & the Radio Padre": letter to James Welch, 11 February 1943.
[120] idem.
[121] ibid., p.40-41.
[122] ibid., p.40.
[123] ibid., p.42.

eloquence. Welch was profoundly moved by the letter and, in particular, by the phrase: "It looks as though, for anything that the Churches have been able to drive into the head of the public, Christ might just as well never have been crucified at all".[124]

James Welch wrote immediately to thank Dorothy for her letter, saying he was "still pondering on it"[125] and stating his conviction that the Religious Broadcasting Department "must consider it seriously in regard to [their] work". He also promised to discuss it in his monthly lunches with William Temple, the new Archbishop of Canterbury and gave it to both Eric Fenn and Cyril Taylor[126] to read. Although no large-scale action was taken for a while, Welch assured Dorothy in April that:

> As some follow up to your letter ... the Radio Padre is trying to put more stuffing into his broadcast talks, and I have been venturing on a series of Lenten sermons ... under the title "The Church has a Story to Tell". But the letter is going to have some effect on all our broadcast work, I hope, because when people ask us what they should preach about, your letter comes as the answer.[127]

In the following few months, mainly as a result of further broadcasts of *The Man Born To Be King* and the publication of the scripts, Sayers received several letters on religious issues from people she had never met. One of these, Mr L. T. Duff, was initially very impolite, saying that he had switched off the third play, "A Certain Nobleman", "in disgust that such drivel should be given over the air"[128] and accusing Dorothy of basing it "on a pack of lies".[129] Surprisingly, considering this inauspicious start, Mr Duff responded positively to Dorothy's extremely caustic reply and, by May, a correspondence had developed which revealed that he was willing to learn more about the Christian faith. Dorothy sent copies of their correspondence to her friends at the Religious Broadcasting

---

[124] ibid., p.40.

[125] Unpublished letter from James Welch to Dorothy L. Sayers, 15 February 1943, Wade Center, File 448/39.

[126] Another colleague at the Religious Broadcasting Department, with particularly responsibility for broadcast services and church music. One of Taylor's first tasks in wartime was to compose the tune Abbot's Leigh to go with the words of "Glorious Things of Thee are Spoken", as the usual tune was, at the time, the same as that of the German national anthem.

[127] Unpublished letter from James Welch to Dorothy L. Sayers, 20 April 1943, Wade Center, File 448/37-38.

[128] *The Letters of Dorothy L. Sayers vol.2: from novelist to playwright*, p.391.

[129] idem.

Department, both to ask their advice and to show them one possible reaction to their work.

Also in May 1943, Dorothy received a typed seven page letter from Stephen Grenfell, a junior employee at the BBC. Despite his initial opinion that *The Man Born To Be King* would be a worthless "dressing up of a rather bedraggled story in a new guise",[130] he had been "deeply affected" by reading the text of the plays. He described himself as one who had cut his teeth "on Wynwood Read, Darwin and Havelock Ellis"[131] and who perceived God as "a powerful administrator but one who, because he was at the head of a job too decentralised for one mind, had made rather a mess of things".[132] Yet, because of the plays, he was ready to pour out all his questions and frustrations to Dorothy Sayers and ask her if she would be prepared to discuss them with him. Dorothy replied with a passionate and beautifully written letter which, although it answers Mr Grenfell's particular questions, could equally well be used as a sermon. While Grenfell had referred to *The Man Born To Be King* as "a cool, satisfying, though fleeting, caravanserai",[133] for Dorothy this description was "a measure of its failure".[134] She declared that "The Gospel is a thing of terror" and reminded her young correspondent that: "God is not just in the caravanserai – though He is there for those who have found Him; He is in the desert, walking to His death".[135] She confronted him with the classic evangelistic choice saying that: "You have got to choose between crucifying God and being crucified with Him: no other choice is open to you or me or any man".[136] She also sent copies of his letter and of her reply to her friends at the Religious Broadcasting Department of the BBC.

Two months later, James Welch returned all the letters, having made several copies, and explained that, as a result of her input, the Religious Broadcasting Department was thinking of having "a sort of unlabelled and unofficial mission"[137] in the first quarter of 1944. He then suggested:

---

[130] Unpublished letter from Stephen Grenfell to Dorothy L. Sayers, 22/23 May 1943, Wade Center, File 411/27.
[131] idem.
[132] idem.
[133] ibid., p.30.
[134] "The Gospel is a Thing of Terror": letter to Stephen Grenfell, 19 June 1943.
[135] idem.
[136] ibid., p.22.
[137] Unpublished letter from James Welch to Dorothy L. Sayers, 12 July 1943, Wade Center, File 448/25.

I'd like, in the fourth broadcast, to ask the question 'What is the Gospel?' and to give as the answer a straightforward reading of your letter to Grenfell, or of most of it, and possibly bits of your reply to Duff (of course no names would be mentioned) ... What would you think about that? [138]

As a result, Dorothy obtained Stephen Grenfell's permission to use their correspondence on the air.

Plans went ahead for the mission during the summer. During this period Dorothy Sayers read two works by Charles Williams which would profoundly affect her: *The Figure of Beatrice*, which would ultimately lead to her translation of Dante's *Divine Comedy*, and "What the Cross Means to Me",[139] a work which Barbara Reynolds affirms "had great meaning for her".[140] Sometime in September, Dorothy was officially informed:

We chose ten preachers with "fire in their bellies" and we have spent forty-eight hours in a retreat-conference with them. They decided to accept the challenge thrown down by your letter.[141]

Welch enclosed a "rough synopsis" of the sermons and a request to tell the Bishops that Dorothy was the person who had motivated their decision to hold the mission in the first place. She replied that he could quote anything he liked to the Bishops as long as he kept her name out of the actual broadcasts. She also provided some pertinent comments on the synopsis.[142]

A month later, things had changed slightly. Welch still wanted to read out word-for-word extracts from Dorothy's letters on the air, but his colleagues were afraid that this would be "a step beyond the ordinary listener".[143] He therefore asked her if she would "write a special letter for such a purpose ... Roughly about 2000-2500 words".[144] How she would have replied in normal

---

[138] idem.

[139] Currently available in *The Image of the City & Other Essays* (First published: OUP 1958), reprinted by Apocryphile Press in 2007.

[140] Barbara REYNOLDS (ed.), *The Letters of Dorothy L. Sayers vol.3, 1944-1950: A Noble Daring*, The Dorothy L. Sayers Society, 1998, p.189.

[141] Unpublished and undated letter (almost certainly the last week of September 1943) from James Welch to Dorothy L. Sayers, Wade Center, File 448/15.

[142] See unpublished letter from Dorothy L. Sayers to James Welch, 2 October 1943, Wade Center, File 448/14.

[143] Unpublished letter from James Welch to Dorothy L. Sayers, 10 November 1943, BBC Written Archives, File 910 2B.

[144] idem.

circumstances to such a request, requiring a lot of extra, unpaid work, we can only guess. However, the following morning Dorothy had what she described as "a sudden illumination". She added:

> It must have been genuine, because the Devil, seeing it come into my mind, was so angry that he overthrew the coffee-pot ... and poured a pint and a half of freshly-made coffee over the gas-grill and the floor and into a small pan of fish-cakes ...[145]

Her letter describing this illumination and commenting on the sermon scripts for the mission is long and very detailed. It is also completely centred on Christ and the Cross which, although Sayers was always christocentric in her theology, shows some traces of the Charles Williams article she had read shortly before this. Three short quotations can sum up the principal message:

> Just go and preach the Gospel at the Market Cross. Never mind the wigs and gloves on the green – the Devil only throws them there to divert people's attention. He doesn't mind what they look at so long as it isn't the Cross.

> Tell them the STORY ... I don't mean the story of the exemplary young carpenter. I mean the story of the act of God in the world.

> You don't really need two thousand words of challenging letter. Five will do: What think ye of Christ?

The Religious Broadcasting Department accepted the genuine nature of the illumination and continued to discuss the mission with Dorothy at length. We have no way of knowing for sure if there is any connection between her less than flattering comments on "the Bishop of Southwark's summary"[146] and the fact that this eminent cleric does not appear in the final list of speakers, but it seems quite probable that there is one. Large parts of James Welch's own talk during the mission were lifted straight out of Dorothy's letters and his introduction to the published talks, entitled *Man's Dilemma and God's Answer*, also contains several quotations from and allusions to the same letters. However, Dorothy's involvement was never made public. She was referred to throughout as "an intelligent listener to religious broadcasts" or "a colleague of mine".[147] We also

---

[145] "The Devil & the Coffee Pot": letter to James Welch, 11 November 1943.
[146] ibid., p.10. The Bishop of Southwark at the time was The Rt Rev. Bertram Fitzgerald Simpson.
[147] James W. WELCH, *Man's Dilemma & God's Answer*, SCM Press, 1944, p.9-18.

learn that Welch had read out the "Radio Padre letter" on the air the Tuesday before the mission started.[148] We may conclude, however, that the mission attracted a lot of interest, as the first published edition of the talks came out in June 1944 and, two months later, was already sold out and had been reprinted.

According to a *Daily Telegraph* editorial as recently as 1996: "religious broadcasting never has matched the quality"[149] of such inspired programmes as those produced in the early nineteen forties under James Welch's leadership. At least part of the credit for this achievement belongs to Dorothy L. Sayers.

A Thought for the Day

The last talk in this volume is much more difficult to place than the others. It clearly was written for the radio on account of the length, the style and the abrupt, shock ending, a standard broadcasting technique and one that Dorothy had used before in the series *Seven Days' Hard*.[150] The title of the original manuscript is "Thought for the Day". However, the daily radio talk of that name did not yet exist at the time it was written. Also, it is not clear whether the title refers to the subject of the talk or to the programme for which it was written. Either is possible as the text is exactly the right length for the programme. However, it may seem a little strange to give the time of a regular feature when you are actually taking part in it.

The predecessor to "Thought for the Day" was a short, specifically Christian, religious broadcast with the official title "Lift up your Hearts – A Thought for To-day", but usually just known as "Lift up your Hearts". It was broadcast every morning at 7.55, just before the 8 o'clock news. It was started in Scotland by Melville Dinwiddie, the Scottish Controller of Programmes of the BBC, in 1939, as a form of "spiritual exercises" when the BBC introduced physical exercises in the early morning for wartime listeners. James Welch liked the idea and extended it to the rest of the United Kingdom. The speakers were usually anonymous, although some of their names were included in the published selections of the talks.[151] The title of the programme was changed to "Thought for the Day" when it was decided to include non-Christian contributors, as "Lift

---

[148] ibid., p.13.
[149] The Daily Telegraph, 12 October 1996.
[150] Broadcast on 3 March 1934.
[151] See *BBC A Thought for To-day: Lift Up Your Hearts* (series 1 to 4), Muller, 1940 to 1942.

up your Hearts", being part of the liturgy, was, as Sayers herself pointed out, "inappropriate to anything but a Christian context".[152]

Another possibility is that Sayers wrote this talk as a "Sunday Postscript". Postscripts in general were originally the work of J. B. Priestley. They lasted for about four minutes straight after the 9 o'clock news at night. The first one, a remarkably moving speech, was broadcast the day after the Dunkirk evacuation, Wednesday 5 June 1940. However, after complaints from the authorities that he was too extreme in his views, too socialist and had a negative effect on morale, Priestley was asked to stop and gave his last Postscript on 20 October 1940, although he continued to broadcast on the overseas service. The programme was then adapted to include other speakers. Some of these, and in particular the *Daily Mirror's* "Cassandra",[153] proved at times much more outrageous.[154] Sunday Postscripts were supposed to have some sort of spiritual or ethical content. We know that Sayers recorded several Sunday Postscripts on Sunday 24 August 1941, although we do not know if these were the first ones she had done. One of these, which was later published in *Unpopular Opinions* as "Living to Work", was largely based on the ninth point of the Church leaders' Manifesto for peace and reconstruction: "The sense of divine vocation must be restored to man's daily work". It had much the same message as James Welch's own "Lift Up Your Hearts" talk on the same Manifesto point, broadcast on 7 March 1941, which had created very little stir, although some of things he said about the other points on other mornings that week provoked a negative parliamentary question from the MP for Hastings.[155] Welch and Dorothy were therefore surprised when the censors objected to her text. A highly confidential BBC internal memo from a Mr Ryan to Welch, which he appears to have shown to Dorothy, states: "It preaches. It digs at mothers, doctors, agriculturalists and capitalists, rather in the manner of a Somerville debating society. It is long-winded".[156] Dorothy herself was officially informed that "it appeared to have political tendencies" and that "our public do not want to be admonished by a woman".[157] She was understandably annoyed.

---

[152] *The Letters of Dorothy L. Sayers vol.3, 1944 – 1950: A Noble Daring*, p.290.

[153] Pen name of the journalist William Connor.

[154] See *The Letters of Dorothy L. Sayers vol.2: from novelist to playwright*, p.276-278, for Sayers' reaction to Cassandra's controversial Postscript about P. G. Wodehouse on 15 July 1941.

[155] See WOLFE, *The Churches & the British Broadcasting Corporation 1922-1956: the Politics of Broadcast Religion*, p.196.

[156] BBC Internal Memo, 26 August 1941, BBC Written Archives, File 910 2A.

[157] Dorothy L. SAYERS, *Unpopular Opinions*, Victor Gollancz, 1946, p.7.

Fixing the date of this talk requires a look at the internal evidence. Sayers refers to a letter published in the press "the other day". It had been written "shortly after the evacuation of Dunkirk", which was finally completed on 4 June 1940. Assuming that no newspaper would publish a letter which had been written more than ten days previously, we can suppose that Sayers' text was composed, and possibly broadcast, during the summer of 1940, which makes it unlikely that this was an official Postscript, as Priestley was still producing nearly all of them at this time. The nearest date to Dunkirk when Sayers spoke on the radio was 21 July 1940. Her short talk, called "And So to Bed", has not been located.[158] We do not know if it was broadcast live or pre-recorded. However, considering the brevity of this talk (the same length as the Thought for the Day text) and the expense of coming to London from her home in Witham, it is highly likely Dorothy would have recorded other, probably similar, things at the same time.

Moreover, it is also possible that this text was not broadcast at all, as it appears to be highly controversial. It is implicitly critical of a man who, although his general attitude does not seem to be particularly full of Christian sentiments, considers that the Dunkirk evacuation was a miraculous answer to prayer and proof that God was pleased with the English people. This understanding of the situation was widespread at the time and even Winston Churchill, who saw himself as a flying buttress rather than a pillar of the Church, because he supported it from the outside, described Dunkirk as "a miracle of deliverance".[159] Therefore, although Sayers greatly admired Churchill, the text could be interpreted as a criticism of his position. The implication, later on in the talk, that no one has the right to expect a miracle, could also be seen as likely to lower morale or to mean that Sayers considered an Allied defeat to be possible.

Although we know very little about this text, its importance for Sayers studies comes from what it tells us about Dorothy's own understanding of faith and divine grace at this period, not to mention her depressing, but probably realistic, analysis of the spiritual state of the nation.

---

[158] It is listed in the BBC Written Archives index cards, but does not appear to be among their microfilm scripts.

[159] See http://news.bbc.co.uk/onthisday/hi/dates/stories/june/4/newsid_3500000/3500865.stm (consulted 20/11/07).

Dorothy Sayers Today

Apart from the joy of reading her lively and entertaining prose, why should we be interested in reading Dorothy Sayers' religious talks today? One of her reasons for writing them in the first place came from her observation that "in the matter of Christian doctrine, a great part of the nation subsists in an ignorance more barbarous than that of the dark ages".[160] This ignorance, combined with the lack of clear and comprehensible documents with which to combat it, led to serious misunderstandings amongst the general public, whose perception of the Christian worldview resembled a "confused jumble of mythological and pathological absurdity".[161] As Dorothy said in picturesque terms to a group of Baptist ministers, "a sour pill of antimacassar morality watered down with saccharine thoughts of mystification and clap-trap".[162] Dorothy often stated that: "If people are to be exhorted to hold the Catholic Faith, it is what G. K. Chesterton calls an 'intellectual convenience' for them to know what the Catholic faith is",[163] and offered this as a justification for her apologetic activities.

Whatever changes in the intellectual climate we can notice since the 1940s, it is certain that an even smaller percentage of the population today is well-informed about Christian doctrine than in Sayers' day and that many people still reject Christianity without having any clear idea of what it is. While Sayers[164] and Lewis[165] estimated the number of practising Christians in Britain in the 1940s at approximately 10% of the population, in September 2006 it was said to be 6.3%.[166] Entertaining and clearly expressed explanations of the basic doctrines of Christianity are just as useful, and difficult to find, now as they were then.

These talks are also essential for our understanding of Dorothy L. Sayers. Most people who know anything at all about her know that she was the author of

---

[160] *The Mind of the Maker,* p.xvii.

[161] idem.

[162] Wade Center File MS 51.

[163] See, for example, *The Letters of Dorothy L. Sayers vol.2: from novelist to playwright,* p.257. G. K. Chesterton actually wrote: "If I am treating man as a fallen being it is an intellectual convenience to me to believe that he fell." (*Orthodoxy,* Harold Shaw, 1994, p.153).

[164] "… nine tenths of the people in this country are ignorant heathen", *The Letters of Dorothy L. Sayers vol.2: from novelist to playwright,* p.119.

[165] "… the Christians are only a tenth part of the population", C. S. LEWIS, *That Hideous Strength,* in *The Cosmic Trilogy,* Pan, 1990, p.655.

[166] See Jonathan PETRE, "Migrants Fill Empty Pews as Britons Lose Faith", *The Daily Telegraph,* 19 September 2006.
http://www.telegraph.co.uk/news/main.jhtml?xml=/news/2006/09/18/nchurch18.xml

a series of twelve plays, called *The Man Born to be King*, which were acclaimed by the Controller of Programmes of the BBC [167] as "one of the great landmarks of broadcasting" [168] and even hailed in *The Listener* as "by far the most remarkable and striking contribution to broadcast drama" [169] ever produced. However, it is less well-known that, as we have seen, the plays, although the longest and most important task she had to accomplish for the Religious Broadcasting Department of the BBC, were part of an ongoing collaboration, which had started in 1938 with the nativity play *He That Should Come* and would continue throughout the war. She worked for many years as script writer, broadcaster and adviser on religious broadcasting. Through this work she made several good friends and worked closely with a group of men with two of whom at least she came to share her deepest religious convictions in way that she was reticent to do with almost anyone else. These scripts, written during the same period as the plays and as *The Mind of the Maker*, add considerably to our knowledge of how Sayers was thinking at the time, enabling us to put her better-known work in context. The letters, in addition to their influence on the 1944 mission, show the depth of Dorothy's desire to see "God incarnate and Christ crucified" [170] preached to the people of Britain.

However, these scripts and letters also allow us to acquire a better grasp of the missionary strategy of James Welch and his team at the Religious Broadcasting Department of the BBC. Even Justin Phillips' excellent study of C. S. Lewis at the BBC, [171] while it does full justice to Sayers' achievement in *The Man Born to Be King*, does not even mention her religious talks. Yet, Sayers' *God the Son* programmes finished less than a month before Lewis's first broadcast talk, [172] and the series on the Creed as a whole was still going on. Both Sayers' and Lewis's contributions were successful parts of Welch and Fenn's overall strategy "to expound the Christian faith in terms that [could] be easily understood by ordinary men and women, and to examine the ways in which that faith [could] be applied" [173] to wartime society. Although Lewis's talks were a great success and the published version, *Mere Christianity*, a huge bestseller, no one could have predicted that at the time. Knowing the immense official reticence about the use of lay people in religious broadcasting, if Dorothy Sayers and T. S. Eliot

---

[167] Mr B. E. Nicholls.
[168] *The Letters of Dorothy L. Sayers vol.2: from novelist to playwright*, p.376.
[169] Alan DENT, "Critic on the Hearth", *The Listener*, 1 April 1943.
[170] See "Christ & the Radio Padre", Letter to James Welch, 11 February 1943.
[171] Justin PHILLIPS, *C. S. Lewis at the BBC*, Harper Collins, 2002.
[172] "Common Decency", broadcast 6 August 1941. Later part of *Mere Christianity*.
[173] James WELCH, *BBC Handbook 1942*, p.59.

had not already proved their ability to speak on Christian themes on the radio, it is unlikely that Lewis would have been asked at all.

In June 1942, James Welch wrote to Dorothy: "We must make you a prophet to this generation and hand you the microphone to use as often as you feel able".[174] She did not feel able very often, being convinced that religious exposition was not her proper job. Other people were not so sure, including Welch, Fenn, C. S. Lewis and the future Cardinal Heenan. One thing is sure; Dorothy did care so much about the religious ignorance of her day that she was, for a short time at least, prepared to play her part in what she called "startling people with the truth".[175] And she did it very well.

SLB
June 2008

---

[174] *The Letters of Dorothy L. Sayers vol.2: from novelist to playwright*, p.364.
[175] Letter to the Bishop of Winchester, 17 March 1942, *The Letters of Dorothy L. Sayers vol.2: from novelist to playwright*, p.356.

Two-part series *Creed or Chaos?*

1. THE CHRIST OF THE CREEDS
Sunday, August 11th 1940

In the title of this talk I will ask you particularly to notice the words: of the Creeds.[1] I am not going to offer you any brand-new theology of my own, nor yet any revolutionary theories belonging to what is called "modern thought". I only want to remind you of something we have been familiar with for so long that we are apt to lose sight of it; namely, what the universal Church thinks, and has always thought, about Christ, and has set down in those formal statements known as the Creeds of the Church. To save argument, I will say now that by "the Church", I mean (for the present purpose) all those bodies of Christians who accept the Creeds as the basis of their doctrine.[2]

And first: a word about the Creeds themselves. They are statements of Christian dogma. That is a word which arouses a good deal of dislike. It is valuable for that very reason, because it makes people sit up and take notice. Actually, a dogma is no more than a considered expression of opinion put forward by authority. This does not mean (as is sometimes supposed) the sort of authority that claps you in gaol if you don't fall in with its notions. It means somebody who has studied the subject and is in a position to pronounce an opinion which we disregard at our own risk. For example, suppose I go to a chemist with a bottle of liquid and ask what it is, and he says: "I can tell you, with all the authority of my professional knowledge, that this is prussic acid, and that if you drink it, you will die." He does not mean that if I disregard this dogmatic opinion and do drink it, he has the authority to have me hanged for disobedience. It means something a good deal more drastic: that if his opinion really is authoritative – if he knows what he is talking about – I shall come into collision with the nature of prussic acid, and condemn myself to death without benefit of judge or jury. In much the same way, the Church says in the Creeds: "This is my authoritative opinion about God and the universe, and I warn you

---

1   Sayers is referring to the Apostles' Creed, the Nicene Creed and the Athanasian Creed.
2   When Sayers was trying to obtain an agreed statement on the "Highest Common Factor" of agreed Christian doctrine, she suggested contacting "the Cardinal [Hinsley], the Anglican Archbishops, the Moderator of the Free Churches, the Moderator of the Church of Scotland (if possible), and the Archbishop of Thyatira" (unpublished letter to James Welch, 22 October 1941, Wade Center File 229). She clearly saw all the bodies represented in this list as part of the universal Church.

that, if you disregard it, you will come into collision with the nature of things, with unhappy results for yourself and society."

Now, what is it exactly that the Church puts forward as her considered opinion about Jesus Christ? First of all, there are the historical facts: that He was born of a particular person, lived on earth, was executed during the term of office of a particular Roman governor, and after His death was seen again in bodily form. These historical details are contained in certain documents which the Church has carefully examined and pronounced to be reliable.[3] (For we must not imagine that the "Higher Criticism"[4] was first invented in the nineteenth century; it was quite familiar to the early Christian authorities who lived close to the events, and who, in fact, rejected as untrustworthy a good many more documents than they accepted, when they put together the books of the New Testament.)

Secondly: On the basis of the historical facts as experienced and examined, the Church has come to a settled opinion about the nature of the man called Jesus. She considers that He was indeed a real man, but that He was, and is, also the Son of God; and she adds, in case this expression should mislead us into thinking that He was something quite different from, or less than, or produced subsequently to, God the Creator, that He is "very God" (that is, "truly God"), that He existed with the Father "before all worlds", and that "by Him all things were made".

What, exactly, does the Church mean us to understand by this? It is important that we should know, because, if Christ was only a man, however noble or amiable, then there is no particular reason for believing what He said or trying to do as He did, than for believing or imitating Diogenes the Stoic, or Good Queen

---

[3]   The four Gospels in the New Testament.

[4]   This term usually refers to the work of a group of German biblical scholars based at the University of Tübingen, Germany, including Friedrich Schleiermacher (1768-1834), David Friedrich Strauss (1808-74), and Ludwig Feuerbach (1804-72), who analysed historical texts from the Middle East in search of independent confirmation of the events related in the Bible and many of whom threw doubt on the historical reliability of the New Testament documents. Their ideas were communicated to England first by Coleridge and then more directly by George Eliot's translations of Strauss's *Life of Jesus* (1846) and Feuerbach's *Essence of Christianity* (1854).
Sayers wrote to the Convenor of the Theological Literature Association on November 28 1941: "Most people still imagine that the "Higher Criticism" has more or less exploded half the Scriptures, and they don't know anything about the results of recent archeological research or textual criticism" (*The Letters of Dorothy L. Sayers vol.2: from novelist to playwright*, p.330). This reference in a radio talk is obviously meant to combat the afore-mentioned misconception.

Bess,[5] or, for that matter, the Emperor Nero or Adolf Hitler. It would just be a matter of what happened to take our fancy. You and I may feel personally that Jesus was a nicer sort of man than Hitler, but that does not give us any assurance that the world will not get on better by following Hitler than by following Jesus. Particularly as Hitler is very much alive, whereas Jesus, if He was only a man, is dead, and not in a position to make His influence very actively felt. But if Jesus Christ is God of God, and made the world to His own pattern, then the situation is very different; for in that case, by disregarding Christ we shall come into collision with the very nature of the universe, and – as we saw about the prussic acid – we defy the nature of things at our peril. Whereas, if we follow Christ, we shall then have the whole universe on our side, and shall be co-operating with the nature of things; particularly, of course, with the true nature of man and of our own selves. In that case, too, Christ is alive and powerful, and we are able to make contact with that great and living power.

It is important, then, that Jesus should be truly God. But if He is so exclusively God that He was never in any real sense an ordinary human being with human limitations like our own, then it is clearly meaningless for us to try and follow in His steps. The conditions that influence us would simply not apply to Him in any way. The whole story of His suffering and death, for instance, would become completely unreal. His body would not be a genuine body, but only a sort of pretence body, like that of a mythical divinity, incapable of death or pain. His intellect would not be like our sort of intellect, that has to learn things, and works upon the general level of contemporary knowledge; it would know everything perfectly at once – the future as well as the past. His emotions would not be our human emotions; he could never experience fear, doubt, surprise, disappointment, courage, hope, or even genuine distress or sorrow; nor would He be subject to any of the passions and temptations which so much complicate your life and mine. Between such a nature and ours there would no more community of experience than between us and a butterfly; He would be starting from a point which we could never hope to reach. In that case, what is more, I fancy we should not think very much of Him as a god, or even as a person, since His whole life and death would be no more than a kind of elaborate play-acting.

The people who think about Christ nearly always tend to sway in one direction or the other. Some of them emphasise the "human Jesus" at the expense of the divine Jesus: they incline to think that he was just a man

---

[5]   Queen Elizabeth I.

33

with a very special awareness of the divine spark that is in all men[6] – a great teacher and prophet, but no more. All those who do not believe in Christ of course take that view – but so do quite a number of those who profess and call themselves Christians.[7] These people accept, that is, the Christian ethics, but not the authority on which those ethics are based. This attitude is understandable, though not really very reasonable. And there are also quite a number of pious people who (without always knowing it), emphasise the divinity of Christ at the expense of His humanity; out of an exaggerated sense of reverence they shrink from the idea that He talked and behaved and was treated by other people like an ordinary human being. They rather give the impression that He never lived in this rough-and-tumble world at all, but always went about in stiff attitudes, like a figure in a stained-glass window, never smiling or joking, and speaking in a special sort of voice, as though He lived permanently in church. I think it is these people who, with the best intentions, antagonise the ordinary man.[8] They make him feel that Christianity is a kind of prim tea-party, reserved for a very respectable and spiritually-minded upper class – quite regardless of the fact that Jesus Himself was notorious for the vulgar and shocking company He kept.[9]

Now the Church in her Creeds will have no truck with either of these attitudes; indeed, she calls them heresies. She insists that Christ was equally and at the same time entirely God and entirely man. The great document which we call the Athanasian Creed – (it is not really a creed, but a commentary on the Creeds) – goes into some detail, in order to make this perfectly clear. After a long passage affirming that God the Son possesses exactly the same divine attributes as God the Father and God the Spirit – that He is uncreated, eternal, illimitable, almighty, and so forth – it goes on to say that when He became the man Jesus He altered nothing of this divine nature, but added to it the nature of a perfect human man. He was altogether God, but also altogether man, with a man's brain and a man's body. It is very positive about this, and, that there

---

[6]   A woman Sayers met during the London production of *The Zeal of Thy House* asked her, referring to the divinity of Christ: "Isn't it the sort of divine spark that there is in all of us, only in a unique degree – the same thing only more so?" (Letter to Father Herbert Kelly, 19 October 1937, *The Letters of Dorothy L. Sayers vol.2: from novelist to playwright*, p.52). Sayers frequently quoted the phrase.

[7]   Allusion to *The Book of Common Prayer*: "…that all who profess and call themselves Christians may be led into the way of truth, and hold the faith in unity of spirit, in the bond of peace…"

[8]   Sayers would later be confronted by this attitude from the members of The Lord's Day Observance Society and The Protestant Truth Society, who opposed the radio production of *The Man Born to Be King*.

[9]   Probably a reference to Matthew 9:10-11.

34

may be no mistake, asserts plainly that though the divine nature in Christ was and is "equal to the Father", the human nature was "inferior to the Father" – subject to God's providence and limited by man's limitations, like every other man that ever lived.

Now, of course, it is all very well to say this; but what does it mean? How can a person be both almighty and limited, both mortal and eternal? What really bogs us here is a failure of the imagination. I will make two suggestions that may be of some help in picturing to ourselves what the Church intends us to understand. First, we may get something out of that useful, though much-abused word, Personality. We may consider that here was a man with the personality of God. I do not mean that God is confined to a human personality – that would be a very crude and anthropomorphic way of looking at it – but rather that this is what God looks like when He is a human person; or that this was God Himself, so far as God can be displayed in human nature. Not a man interpreting God, as a critic's commentary interprets Shakespeare, but rather, as it were, like Shakespeare's plays themselves, which are Shakespeare, just so far as Shakespeare's mind can be incarnated in ink and paper. The plays, that is, are not the whole of Shakespeare, but they are wholly and uniquely Shakespeare, and the means above all others by which we can get in touch with Shakespeare's personality. Other plays, benefiting by the example and inspiration of the incarnate Shakespeare, may be written, as we say, "in a Shakespearian manner", or "in the Shakespearian spirit", but they cannot be said, like Shakespeare's own plays, to be Shakespeare. In a similar way, all men have something of the divine spirit in them, but only Christ was the divine personality.

My other suggestion is about the union of the divine and human in Christ. Once again, our chief difficulty is to imagine it. In the Gospel accounts, we get moments in which Christ seems to speak and act like an ordinary man – He is meek and lowly, anxious and troubled, daunted by the prospect of death and failure – he seems conscious only of our common humanity. But at other times, we get glimpses of something very strange indeed – a whirlwind of power, speaking with authority, and asserting the paramount importance of His own person with an arrogance unparalleled in history; at such times He behaves as though He were God, and knew Himself to be God. How are we to reconcile these two Christs into one consistent personality? There is a purely human parallel which may, I think, assist our imagination, and that is the man possessed of that fiery and especial power which we call genius. Such a man knows perfectly well the kind of being that he is. Make no mistake about that. It is not consciously in his mind every time he says, "pass the mustard",[10] but that knowledge is always subconsciously with him – it is an unspoken assumption by which he orders his whole life. And every so often, when something happens which challenges that fundamental reality, his certain knowledge of himself breaks upward into consciousness, and he thunders out his tremendous self-assertion; I AM THAT I AM.[11] So too, the human Jesus, the teacher, the prophet, the carpenter's son responds to the challenge of His divinity: "Thou art the Christ, the Son of the living God"[12] – "Blessed art thou, Simon Bar-Jonah". "Art thou a king?"[13] – "I am". "Thou art not yet thirty years old, and thou hast seen Abraham?" – "Before Abraham was, I AM."[14]

These two suggestions are, of course, mere illustrations, and no part of Church doctrine or dogma. The Church contents herself with asserting the divine-human nature, but leaves Christians perfectly free to imagine anything they like about it, provided they keep firmly in their minds both the Godhead and the Manhood. A mere approval of Christian morals, or a patronising recognition of a very superior human type will not do; nor yet a vague sense of spiritual uplift in the presence of something supernatural; neither of these is Christian, in the Church's sense of the word. A man must not only believe, but believe rightly, and understand what it is he believes. The curious popular notion that religion means a hazy "spirit of belief" in nothing in particular is one for which the Church has no use at all. She thinks it quite irrational; and if irrational, then unchristian, since, if Christ is God, then He is the very embodiment of the divine Reason itself. If anyone intends to "believe in" Christ, he ought, she feels, to make up his mind why.

The Church's own belief – that Christ was both God and man – has certain important consequences for human life. For one thing, it implies that religion

---

[10] Dorothy Sayers created some well-known advertisements for Colman's Mustard while she was working for Benson's advertising agency in London.

[11] Allusion to Exodus 3:14.
In the article "Divine Comedy", first published in March 1940, Sayers had imagined a producer talking to the actor playing the role of Jesus: "Well, yes, I suppose you know you're God all the time, but surely not in that rigid, theological sense. I should think it would be more like the way a man knows deep down inside him he is really a genius. It's the unspoken assumption on which he habitually acts, but it isn't perpetually present to his conscious thought." (*Unpopular Opinions*, Gollancz, 1946, p.22-23.)

[12] Matthew 16:16.

[13] John 18:37.

[14] John 8:58. – Actually Dorothy's memory was at fault here. The biblical text says: "fifty years old".

is concerned, not merely with what happens in the spiritual world, or what becomes of us after death, but also, with what happens here and now in this world; it is concerned with society, as well as with the individual soul. It is active, positive, and creative; a Christian's business is not just to sit about being good, but to go about doing good.

Further, in affirming that God was made flesh, the Church affirms that matter and the material body are good and not evil. The fear and hatred of matter and the body are not orthodox Christianity; they belong to a very ancient and very tough and enduring heresy – the heresy of the Manichees.[15] I hope to say something about this next week. In this and in other respects it is, of course, open to anybody to reject the Church's opinion; but whether we accept it or reject it, it is, I think, always a convenience to know what that opinion actually is.

2. THE SACRAMENT OF MATTER
Sunday, 18th August 1940

From what we said last week about the Christian doctrine of the union of God and man in the person of Christ, it follows that Christianity is bound to be a sacramental religion. The word "sacrament" is one of those controversial expressions that people get extremely heated about; but I will ask you, for the moment, to put resolutely out of your thoughts all the disputes about transubstantiation, infant baptism, the validity of English orders,[16] and whether the confessional is a means of divine Grace, or a kind of secret weapon for the corruption of manners and the enslavement of the population. Before we can begin to consider all that, we have to clear up a preliminary question: What is the nature of a sacrament as such?[17]

---

[15] A key belief in Manichaeism, based on the teachings of the prophet Mani (c.210-276 AD), is that there is no omnipotent good power. Manichees explain the problem of evil by denying the infinite perfection of God and postulating two equal and opposite powers. Each individual human is seen as a battleground for these powers: the good part is the soul (composed of light) and the bad part is the body (composed of dark earth). Mani also declared himself to be the Paraclete or Comforter promised by Jesus Christ.

[16] The longstanding argument about the Roman Catholic refusal to accept the validity of Anglican ordination.

[17] Sayers wrote to Father Kelly: "There is a deep-rooted conviction in most people's minds that Sacraments are magic, working *ex opere operato*" (*The Letters of Dorothy L. Sayers vol.2: from novelist to playwright*, p.48). Her definition attempts to firmly quash this misunderstanding.

The distinctive thing about a sacrament is that it prescribes, in addition to a spiritual feeling, some kind of bodily act: in the Eucharist, the eating and drinking of bread and wine; in baptism, the washing with water, and so on. It is not the same thing as a symbol. An inn sign may be a symbol of good fellowship; the pledging of a friend's health is not only a symbol, but a sacrament of good fellowship. There must, that is, be three things present before we can call any act "sacramental" – the right material means, the right words, and the right intention. Thus, in the case of the drinking of healths, the health must be drunk <u>in</u> something – there must be real wine (or tea, or lemonade, or barley-water, according to the ritual adopted); there must be words expressive of your wishes, such as "Here's how", or "Good luck", or what not; and there must be the right intention – you must be sincere in your wish, otherwise, you are committing yourself to a solemn and public lie, and the thing is not a sacrament, but a sacrilege. So, too, with the Church's sacraments. There are the material means – the water or the bread and wine – there are the prescribed ritual words, but these must not be a mere formality – there <u>must</u> also be the right intention. Contrary to what many people suppose, the Church insists just as strongly on the intention as on the words and the material means. Exactly as she is firm about the completely divine <u>and</u> the completely human nature in Christ, so she is firm about the physical and mental part of the sacrament on the one hand <u>and</u> the spiritual part of it on the other. And for the same reason. Her sacraments are her way of maintaining before the world that central meaning of the Incarnation – the intimate and unbreakable union of spirit with mind and matter.

Let us get this quite clear, because it is so important. The story of the life of Christ is not a symbolic story, like the legends of the heathen gods. The heathen gods were not real people, though the tales about them often typify or symbolise important religious truths. But the Incarnation of Christ is not a symbol, but a sacrament, because He was a real man, and the events of His life were real events in history. He was not only God, but God in a material body, and with a rational mind in a material brain. His Incarnation was a supreme and particular instance of the close sacramental union of spirit and matter throughout the universe; and the sacraments also are solemn and particular occasions of that same universal union.

Of course you may say, "Why have particular seasons and occasions? I can feel full of kindliness to my neighbours without treating them to ritual drinks. And I can worship God without sacraments, and without going to church." Well, so you can – and you can also, no doubt, love your wife without ever telling her so, or showing her any signs of affection; but that is not a very natural way of going on. It is strange that the sacraments of the Church should so often be attacked for being something mysterious, unnatural and unnecessary, when our whole daily life so readily takes on little sacramental forms. The good-bye kiss on the platform, the asking of one's friends to dinner, the presentation of birthday gifts (when, as Humpty-Dumpty said, there are so many days in the year when one can receive unbirthday presents [18]), the letting off of fireworks on November 5th [19] – all these things bear witness to the fact that ordinary human nature, being a part of the material universe spread out in space and time, naturally turns to special times, places and material means for the expression of its spiritual longings and the satisfaction of its spiritual needs. The Church never runs against the grain of the universe, but always with it; she never contradicts the nature of things, but always strongly upholds it.

Yet behind these objections that some people feel to set times and formal ceremonies, there lies the shadow of a great truth, namely, that in us, matter and spirit are so intimately bound up that there is not any action of our lives that may not be called in some sense sacramental. That which we call soul or spirit is almost incapable of realising itself, and quite incapable of communicating itself to others, except by some bodily means. Apart from those few rare people who, by long practice and training, are able, for short periods, to escape from their material surroundings and enter into direct awareness of the spiritual world, the highest functions of the ordinary man, whether he is loving or praying, are carried out by, with, and in the body. The Christian Church, far from deploring this, or thinking there is something wrong about it, contends that this is, in fact, the right and normal way to go to work. Unlike the Buddhist religion, for example, which withdraws the soul perpetually within itself and away from the world of matter, the Christian religion works from within outward, drawing more and more of the world of matter within its own orbit. We sometimes tend, for instance, to think of prayer as a purely spiritual experience, involving only God and the individual soul. Actually, it involves the body as well. When we think about God, we are using our material brain; when we say our prayers in words, we are using our material tongues; when we fall on our knees or clasp our hands, we are using our whole bodies to pray with; when we unite in prayer with other people, we are adding the power of their material presence to our own; if we are Catholics, we are ready to go farther

---

[18] Lewis CARROLL, *Through the Looking Glass*, chapter 6.
[19] To celebrate the failure of the Gunpowder Plot to blow up the Houses of Parliament with King James I and all the members of the Lords and Commons in them on November 5th 1605.

– we may light a candle and set it up in church. It is a mistake to suppose that this is idle superstition; it is an assertion that we can pray with the very stuff of the universe itself – that the entire world of matter is the temple of God and the temple of our own souls, and a proper instrument with which to worship its divine Creator.

But what justification have we got to any such tremendous assertion? We know very well that material things are apt to be a snare and a delusion. Preachers are, indeed, continually warning us against putting our trust in the body and in material things, and sometimes the struggle between the spirit and the body is so hard that we are inclined to think that there must be something evil about the material universe as such. Many people imagine that the Church actually takes this point of view, and some of them are violently opposed to her on the ground that she is always wanting to deny and degrade the body.

Now we must say, straight away, and without possibility of misunderstanding, that any doctrine which maintains that matter is evil in itself is entirely heretical and entirely un-Christian. The Church does not say that matter is evil, nor that the body is evil. For her very life, she dare not. For her whole life is bound up in the doctrine that God Himself took human nature upon Him and went about this material world as a living man, with a human body and a human brain, and that he was perfect and sinless in the body as out of the body, in time as in eternity, in earth as in heaven. That is her creed; that is her dogma; that is the opinion to which she stands committed. If she were for one moment to admit that matter and body were in themselves evil things, she would blast away the very foundations of her existence and utterly destroy herself. For her, matter is so good that God could make Himself a part of it, and take no hurt to His perfection, nor to His holiness.

And this is, indeed, the great union commemorated and renewed in all the sacraments of the Church – the union of God with matter. It is not an unnatural union of two things violently opposed; nor does it mean that God is ever absent from His material universe – any more than your love is ever absent from your children and friends; it is like a solemn and sacramental kiss of union: in the words of the English catechism, "a means whereby we receive the same, and a pledge to assure us thereof".[20]

Matter is not itself evil. It is true that it can be made evil – but that is not

---

[20] Found in the 1662 *Book of Common Prayer*.

a special peculiarity of matter; it is true of the spirit also. There are dark and terrible sacraments of evil as well as sacraments of good, and when the body of matter is united to the spirit of evil, it becomes a very dangerous weapon indeed. St Augustine of Hippo, who himself had a good deal of trouble in the flesh, has put in a nutshell the Christian attitude to the material universe. "If bodies delight thee, praise God for them, and reflect thy love upon their Maker, lest, in what pleases thee, thou shouldst displease Him. If souls delight thee, let them be loved in God: for they too are changeable and go their way, and perish, unless fixed and established in Him. Let them be loved, then, in Him."[21]

Now, this doctrine of the sacramental nature of matter and mind has consequences which we do not always fully realise. All abuse of matter, or of body and mind, is sacrilege, and a crucifixion of the body of Christ. This is not confined to what the Church of England calls, "open and notorious evil living".[22] It means all abuse. All cruelty to God's living children, all greedy exploitation of the world's resources, all waste and destruction, all using of matter for ugly and evil ends. To burn the crops or let them rot, because it does not pay to transport them to the men and women who need them, is sacrilege against God and sacrilege against His universe. The abuse of men and machines to make useless and undesirable goods for profit is sacrilege. The enslavement of men's minds and bodies by tyrannous forms of government is sacrilege – it is the binding and the scourging of the body of God. Still further: all denial of human reason is sacrilege; all wilful stupidity is sacrilege; it is the denial of the mind of God. All bad art is sacrilege; it is the torturing of matter into ugly and unnatural forms, and a treason against the divine beauty. All jerry-building or dishonest workmanship is sacrilege; it is introducing a lie into the body of Christ. And every sin against society is sacrilege, because we are all members one of another, in that material body which is the body of the living God.

The abuse of man, and the abuse of matter – we can see today to what desperate straits this sacrilege has led us. The Church maintains that all these disastrous judgements are the result of wrong beliefs, which have caused us to

---

[21] *The Confessions of St Augustine*, Book IV.

[22] Only a clergyman found guilty of "open and notorious evil living" could, according to the rubrics of the Church of England, be removed from his responsibilities. Equally, an "open and notorious evil liver" could be asked by his parish clergy not to come forward to take the bread and wine at a service of Holy Communion. Nowadays the usual expression in the same context is "conduct unbecoming".

run counter to the very nature of the universe. God never punishes anybody for wrong beliefs – He leaves them to punish themselves. Unless a man believe rightly, he cannot – and with the best will in the world he <u>cannot</u> – be saved.[23] But if he believes rightly, then God and the universe are fighting upon his side, and the gates of hell shall not prevail against him.[24]

---

[23] An allusion to the words of the Athanasian Creed.
[24] Matthew 16:18.

THE RELIGIONS BEHIND THE NATION

Broadcast on March 5th 1941

It is comparatively easy to say that we want to defend our civilisation and recover our culture. But what *is* our culture? How did we come by it? What is it based on? What distinguishes it from the thing we call barbarism? And – perhaps the most disquieting question of all – is that culture really something in the power of which we live and die, or is it merely a slogan we repeat in order to persuade ourselves that there is something in this country worth living and dying for?

It has been said that what determines the culture of a people is its religious outlook. That statement would, of course, be disputed by a number of people – especially those who imagine that cultural progress consists in gradually getting rid of religion in favour of scientific enlightenment and a realistic interpretation of history. But these people do not, I think, quite realize what the statement actually means. It means this: *that the kind of culture we make for ourselves depends upon the assumptions we hold in common about what is GOOD.*

The assumptions. Not the doctrines we preach, not the things we seek to establish by argument, but the things we take so much for granted that we never argue about them at all. The preconceptions so ingrained in us that we do not realise our dependence on them until we hear them challenged; so sacred to us that when they *are* challenged, we are too shocked to argue back and can only cry out as though at a blasphemy.

For example: we *take it for granted* that all man and all races possess certain rights in common, just because they are men. We take it for granted that such things as freedom, mercy, charity, truth, tolerance, justice and peace are Good Things. Though here and there we may fail to practise, or disagree about how best to practise, these virtues, we conduct our private and public lives, and base all our arguments, on the assumption that they *are* virtues. When the Nazis simply *deny* these assumptions – when they base their New Order of civilisation on the contrary assumptions that inferior races have no rights, that mercy and charity are effeminate vices, and that war is more desirable than peace, we are not merely horrified, we are plainly incredulous. We don't believe what they say. To us, such a civilisation would be no civilisation at all, but sheer barbarism.

What we are making, you see, is a set of assumptions about the *nature of*

43

the good; and to these assumptions we all cling desperately – not least, those believers in scientific rationalism who claim that all speculation about the nature of the good should be swept away into the limbo reserved for metaphysics and religious superstition. Take, for example, the still very popular idea of human progress. Originally, this was bound up with biological theories about evolution. Although biological evolution offers practically no evidence of any kind of *moral* progress in the natural world, we passionately take it for granted that man's progress *must* be in the direction of moral perfection; if it was anything else, we should *refuse* to call it progress. On that the evolutionists and the rationalists are agreed: the more man develops and the more knowledge he acquires, the better he must become – *better*, in the sense that he must become more and more free, merciful, just, truthful, and so on, conforming more and more closely to our ingrained assumptions about the nature of the good. Nobody – not even the most anti-religious of our thinkers – would seriously suggest that a fully-developed and fully enlightened humanity might prove to be wholly cruel, violent, base, tyrannical, and false.

But why? What makes us so sure about this?

The fact is that at the very basis of our thought and behaviour there lies a pair of assumptions which are wholly religious – which reason cannot prove and for which science can offer no evidence. We assume that *both* our conception of the good *and* our human reason are really valid. We assume, that is, *first*, that the universe *makes sense*, so that when we try to interpret it rationally, we can trust our own reasoning so far as it goes. We assume, secondly, that the universe has a purpose and *that its purpose is good* – in other words, that our recognition of certain qualities as good really does correspond in some way with the fundamental reality of things.

Now, how do we come to make these assumptions? There is nothing new about the ideas themselves. At all times and in all places, thinking men have distinguished a particular set of virtues which we may call the 'humane' virtues, and have claimed high places for them in the name of sovereign reason; again and again such thinking men have fought against the suggestions that the world was governed by pure force or mere irrational chance.

To go no further back than the era which immediately preceded our own in Europe: the great and splendid pagan civilization of Rome had reasoned out for itself an ideal of social perfection very like our own. Two thousand years ago, the greater part of the known world was held together in the security of an established order and in the enjoyment of a culture based on humane virtues and rationalized by an enlightened secular philosophy.

Yet the Roman civilization collapsed, as the civilization of Greece had collapsed before it. It crumbled away at the circumference and it rotted away at the centre; and when the challenge of the Barbarians came, Rome could not find that burning faith and confidence in herself that could have inspired her to defend her culture against aggression. She was, indeed, rather in the mood of the Western Democracies at the beginning of the present war – she had become not quite sure what she stood for; or rather, she felt she did stand for some sort of world-wide human solidarity, based on reason and virtue, but she had grown to doubt whether there was any warrant in fact or theory for believing that such a solidarity was real or possible.

The fact is – and we may as well face it – that the enlightened human reason can establish almost anything except those two basic suppositions on which a human culture depends: it cannot *prove* that goodness is not an illusion, and it cannot *prove* that reason itself is not an illusion. So the enlightened ancient world, brought up against the hard knocks of actual fact, took refuge in an idealist philosophy – truth, mercy, order, beauty, righteousness – all these things might be cherished as ideals, but *only* as ideals. They were states of perfection, but they were unattainable by man – true only of the blessed gods. And the gods themselves were personifications of these ideals, myth and allegory and no more. There was no contact between human and divine; no assurance that the ideal corresponded in any way with human experience.

The power that came to regenerate Rome – though only at the cost of shattering the whole structure of her civilization to pieces – was Christianity. It did not save Rome from the Barbarians – but it built on the ruins of the old Rome a new and living Rome that included and absorbed Barbarism. Christian dogma, indeed, proved the one thing tough enough to pull Europe through the dark ages that followed the collapse of the pagan philosophers. Yet it proclaimed no new truths. It was not the denial of the old religions, but their fulfilment. It asserted that the things which man had believed about right and reason from the beginning of time, were neither idle dreams nor wishful thinking, but actually and earthily true as the everlasting hills. It claimed in fact:

First: that man's persistent belief in goodness and reason were justified; that such was the nature of God and the true nature of man – and that Christ was there to prove it.

Secondly: that the things men called good were valid, not merely in some remote ideal heaven, but here and now, because the Kingdom of God was come already.

Thirdly: that although men could never achieve perfection by their own efforts, there was a real link between God and man in the person of Christ who was God and man at once.

Thus Christianity offered the actual physical fact of the Incarnation as, first, a *guarantee* that right and reason were valid, and, secondly, a *means* whereby the perfection that was impossible with man was made possible by God. For, in asserting that the Divine Reason and Goodness had actually taken human nature at a particular date and in a particular place, Christianity took theology out of the realm of myth and allegory, and pegged it firmly down to history. It picked up, so to speak, all the scattered ideas about God and man and the universe which had been lying about like loose beads – beautiful but disconnected – and ran through them, like a string, the historical personality of the God who was made flesh.

It is the pattern of those beads on that string that is the pattern of our own civilization and culture. We have grown accustomed to the look of it. We have spent nineteen and a half centuries polishing the beads. And during that time, we have been tempted to feel that the only thing that spoils the look of them is the ugly string of Christian dogma running through them. For the last three centuries, we have been snipping the string away, strand by strand – forgetting that it was the string that made the pattern in the first place. Let us be quite clear about that. The assumptions we take for granted about right and reason, and which seem to us self-evident, are not self-evident at all. After nineteen and a half centuries of Christianity, they have become a mental habit with us; but the *evidence* for them is the evidence for Christianity, and if we reject the one we automatically reject the other. What we have been trying to do for some time is to keep the Christian ethic without the connecting thread of Christian theology – the beads without the string. We can, of course, hope or imagine that the pattern will hold together of its own accord, but we have no rational warrant for supposing that it will; indeed, the witness of history contradicts that supposition.

What is more, the separate beads, when detached from the string, roll away into very odd corners and do some very queer things. Freedom, for example, when it is made an absolute good-in-itself and is no longer interpreted as freedom to behave in accordance with the divine pattern for man. It becomes the absolute freedom of the individual to behave unsocially; absolute freedom of speech to talk any mischievous and lying nonsense; the absolute freedom of money to exercise uncontrolled power. Freedom set loose from the bond of theology brings us up against that ugly paradox: 'The freedom of the strong may mean the bondage of the weak, and the freedom of the many, the bondage of the good.' The logical consequence of absolute freedom is absolute tyranny.

Or consider peace, conceived as the immediate good-in-itself – not as a spiritual condition, but as a political aim, and consisting in the bare absence of bloodshed. We have seen what that produces: on the one hand, sloth, timidity, reluctance to interfere with persecution and injustice; on the other hand, the triumph of force by way of threats, blackmail, perjury, and the whole 'sickening technique'[1] of oppression, till a peace so maintained became intolerable – and the logical result of total peace is seen to be total war.

We have seen, too, what happens to reason divorced from theology. Encouraged by its success in subduing the material universe, it refuses to admit the validity of anything that is not capable of scientific *proof*. Its next step is to try to justify the natural virtues by their material results – whence we get the ugly and egotistical doctrine of enlightened self-interest and the hideous tyranny of economics. The *last* achievement of reason is always to cast doubt on its own validity: so that the final result of rationalism is the appearance of a wholly irrational universe.

Thus, human ethics, left to themselves, become helpless and self-contradictory – exactly as they did in pagan times.

The men who now rule Germany, having thrown over the Christian theology, see clearly enough that the Christian ethics will not work without it. Therefore, they have jettisoned the ethics as well. We are greatly shocked by this. But have we the right to be surprised? If Christ is the only guarantee that reason is rational and goodness is good, then, the logical result of repudiating Christianity is the repudiation of reason and virtue.

---

[1] This is a reference to Prime Minister Neville Chamberlain's speech to the House of Commons on September 1st 1939, denouncing the Nazi invasion of Poland. Chamberlain said: "We have no quarrel with the German people except that they allow themselves to be governed by a Nazi Government. As long as that Government exists and pursues the methods it has so persistently followed during the last two years, there will be no peace in Europe. We shall merely pass from one crisis to another, and see one country after another attacked by methods which have now become familiar to us in their sickening technique."

We are not ready to go so far as this. But we are left in a state of *neutrality* – neither vigorously Christian nor boldly anti-Christian; unwilling to give up Christian ethics, but unable to assert them positively because we can no longer give any good grounds to justify our faith in them. We are, as has well been said, 'living on our Christian capital'.

Or we might say that we are at present on the defensive – fighting a desperate and bewildered rearguard action, cut off from our spiritual reinforcements. We cannot do that for ever. We must know what we are fighting about and what we are fighting for. And it will be well that we should begin by grasping this plain fact: that we can make no intelligent and wholehearted fight for our 'European culture' unless we are also ready to fight for the Christendom upon which that culture (whether we realise it or not) is founded.

GOD THE SON

1. Lord & God

BBC Forces Programme: Sunday 8th June 1941: 2.50 - 3.00 pm London

"I believe in one Lord Jesus Christ, the only-begotten Son of God, begotten of the Father before all worlds."

Today we come to the second main division of the Creed. It begins very oddly – if the words were not so familiar to us we should notice at once how exceedingly odd they are.[1] The Creed has been talking about the eternal nature of God in Heaven; but suddenly, in the middle of all this, it makes a kind of swoop or dive into human history, picks out the name of a Jewish carpenter living in the reign of Tiberius Caesar and known to his contemporaries as Jesus, and then, without a word of explanation or so much as a pause for breath, swoops up again out of time and space into Heaven and eternity and goes on talking about God. Only, this time, it talks about Him under the name of Jesus the carpenter; "one Lord Jesus Christ, the only begotten Son of God, begotten of His Father before all worlds, God of God ………. By whom all things were made."

This, come to think of it, is very startling; we might be excused for supposing that the Church had got mixed up in her dates. She seems to assert blandly that the world was made by somebody who was not born till a rather late date in the world's history; which sounds rather contradictory. Besides, she began by saying that the world was made by God; what then has the man Jesus got to do with it? We beg the Church to express herself a little more clearly. The Church replies, unabashed: "I will explain all that in a minute or two. For the moment I am still talking about the power by which the world was made, and I assure you that for this purpose it is quite immaterial whether I use the great name of God or the name of Jesus the Carpenter: they are one and the same." In fact, this extraordinary juggling with time and place, this sudden jerking of a man's name into the middle of a statement about the nature of God, is the

---

[1]   On April 1st 1941, in a seven page long letter, Eric had suggested that Sayers start her series "straight off with a question: Has it ever struck you how very oddly the Creed starts off its second main division?" She wrote "Children's Hour touch!" in the margin and replied: "I'm *not good* at the direct personal appeal – 'Has it ever struck you –?' … Flat statement and argument is my natural line, and I shall make a ghastly mess of the other if I try it." (*The Letters of Dorothy L. Sayers vol. 2: from novelist to playwright*, p.244.)

Church's dramatic way of establishing the great central doctrine of the Christian faith: that Jesus Christ, the Son of God, is both God <u>and</u> Man.

Having made an urgent note, as it were, of this, as something to be examined later on, the Creed leaves it there. So we will leave it too, and ask next what is meant by saying that besides God the Father there is also a divine being called the "Son of God" or "God the Son", who is "begotten of His Father before all worlds".

We must not be misled by the expressions "Son" and "begotten". In this connection they have nothing to do with the birth <u>in</u> the world of the man Jesus; nor do they mean that God the Father came first and that God the Son was somehow produced later on. These words are symbols, or picture-words, which try to convey that within the eternal Mind, or Spirit, or Power that lies beyond this world of space, time and matter, there is something which we may call a distinction without a difference. We might say that there are two fields of force, or two rallying points of the power: but because the great being of God includes everything we understand by the word "personality", the Church calls them two "persons",[2] the Father and the Son. <u>Like</u> a father and son, they are distinct from one another, yet <u>like</u> a father and son, they share the same nature, and <u>like</u> a father and son, they are united in mutual love. But <u>unlike</u> a human father and son, neither of them can be called older or more important or more powerful than the other, and each is so perfectly the exact image and expression of the other that they are actually one and the same Mind, Power, and Spirit.

This sounds very mysterious and difficult; but we can find something rather like it in our own experience. St John has another symbol or picture for God the Son – he calls Him "God the Word" – "in the beginning was the Word, and the Word was <u>with</u> God and the Word <u>was</u> God."[3] Let us see what we can do with that.

Suppose you have an idea – a thought – in your mind; let us take quite a simple thought: you think, "I should like a cigarette". As you think the thought,

---

[2] Sayers was very wary of using the word "persons" to describe the Trinity. She wrote to D. G. Jarvis on October 18 1940: "the word "Person" ... does not mean, theologically, what it means in every-day English – i.e. an entirely separate *character*, but is a (not very happy) translation of the Greek *hypostasis*, meaning, rather, a distinct *mode of being*." (*The Letters of Dorothy L. Sayers vol.2: from novelist to playwright*, p.185.)

[3] John 1:1.

the words come into your mind. You cannot say that there is no distinction between the word and the thought – and yet the words are the exact expression of the thought: they are the very means by which you become aware of that thought and convey it to other people; and it is true in a sense that the word and the thought come into existence together and are really one and the same thing. As soon as you had the thought, you had the words for it: you might put it into picture-language and say that the thought immediately begot the words. So St John's image of God the Word helps us to understand what is meant by the expression that the Son is begotten of the Father "from everlasting" or "before all worlds". We are to think of two persons being related in one way like a father and a son, and in another way like the thought and the word – two different pictures to express one and the same truth.[4]

Picture words are also very valuable in expressing truth, but we are apt to let the picture run away with us that it is often advisable to have two quite different pictures of the same thing to act as a check on one another. If we think all the time of "The Father and the Son", we may end up believing that God the Father really is a white-haired old gentleman sitting on a golden throne high up in the clouds, and that God the Son is just the human Jesus and no more. If, on the other hand, we think all the time of the Thought and the Word, we may end up by imagining that God is nothing but a collection of abstract ideas, without any personal qualities such as love, or mercy, or joy, or beauty. But if we think sometimes one way and sometimes the other, we may get a more balanced and complete idea of what the Church means us to understand about God.

Now our words are very often inadequate and contradictory. They are seldom the perfect expression of our thought. But God the Word is the perfect expression of God's mind – nothing about the Word is incomplete or contradictory or out of tune with the Thought. In other words, the Son "does the Will of the Father", and does it perfectly. God does not fumble and contradict himself. In whatever varied ways He expresses Himself – in all His material works, and in the hearts of men, as in the innermost mystery of His eternal being – He is single and unchanging. That is why the Church speaks of God the Word as the only-begotten Son of God. And we have to bear in mind that this divine Word, the perfect expression of God's mind, is also that same Jesus who, when He was on earth, said that He had come "to do the will of the Father".

---

[4] This is a simplified version of the analogy developed in *The Mind of the Maker*, which Sayers had recently finished writing, where the Trinity is likened to the Idea, the Energy and the Power.

So, if we say this short passage of the Creed again, we shall see that it gives to God the Son three separate titles: "Lord", "Jesus", and "Christ" – one Lord Jesus Christ. The first word, "Lord", tells us that He is really and perfectly God: and we shall talk about this again next week. The second word, "Jesus", tells us that He was really and truly a man, and we shall deal with this in the two following Sundays. The third word, "Christ", tells us what part this Lord Jesus, God and Man, plays in human history; my last two talks will just touch on this, but it will be treated much more fully by later speakers when they come to the passages in the Creed which have to do with God the Holy Ghost and with the work of the Church.

2. Lord of all Worlds

Forces: Sunday 15th June 1941: 2.50 - 3.00 pm

"God of God, Light of Light, very God of very God; begotten not made; being of one substance with the Father; by whom all things were made."

Last week we started to examine what the Creed says about the Second Person of the Godhead – the person whom, when we think about his short life on earth, we call Jesus, Son of God, and, when we think about his eternal life in Heaven, we call God the Son. The next passage goes on to affirm, with more emphasis and in more detail, that this Person is believed by the Church to be really and truly God – every bit as much God as God the Father Himself. He is "God of God, Light of Light, very (that is, true) God of True God". The Creed from which these words are taken was drawn up at Nicaea in the year 325, and its special object was to clear away all possible misunderstanding about this part of the Christian Faith. At the time there were many people, just as there are today, who thought that Jesus was just a very good man, with only the same kind of likeness to God that is in every man, though perhaps rather more so. Others thought He was perhaps a real god of sorts, but inferior to God the Father – something like the lesser deities imagined by the Greeks and Romans. That is why we get this insistent hammering on the one point. The Son is not made – God did not create Him as he created the universe. The Son is begotten of God as the word is begotten of the thought which it expresses. He is God of God – springing or arising out of God, true God of true God – not a demi-god or a myth. Finally, so that there shall be no possible mistake about it, we get that famous phrase which rent Christendom asunder before it was generally accepted, "being of one substance with the Father".

"Of one substance" – not merely "of like substance". In the original Greek in which the Nicene Creed was written there is between those two phrases the difference of only one letter – the Greek letter *iota*, the little letter "i". "Of like substance": *homoiousion* with an "i"; "of one substance": *homoousion* without the "i". In the fierce and bloody controversy that raged before the supporters of the letter "i" were branded as heretics and driven out of the Church, all Christendom was split for an *iota*. But the quarrel about that "i" was not, as shallow-minded people like to pretend, a foolish squabble among pedants about a technicality. On the absence or presence of the "i" there hung the whole difference between God and man, between Heaven and earth. Men fought and bled for those words;

the great bishop Athanasius faced exile and persecution and death, not once but many times, rather than consent to pronounce that single letter. For that word *homoousion*, "of <u>one</u> substance", is the word that pins down belief to the central doctrine of Christianity in a way that admits of no shuffling or misunderstanding. It is the acid test that distinguishes true Christianity from the various forms of modified or near-Christianity. It is the uncompromising assertion that the Lord Jesus is not a mere man, not a mere myth or demi-god, not a mere symbol of religious emotion, but actually and personally, on earth as in Heaven, the one Lord God Almighty.

The word "substance", by the way, needs a little explanation. Here it is a technical term, which may be rather misleading to us now, though its meaning was quite plain to those who first used it. Today, we use "substance" to mean two different and quite opposite things. It may mean "material stuff", thus, for example, we might say that our daily newspaper and the Bible were both made of the same substance, namely, paper and ink. But this is not what we mean when we talk of the "substance" of a book or document. The "substance" of a newspaper leader is not by any means the "substance" of a chapter of St John's Gospel, whatever material they may be printed on. On the other hand, the "substance" of a particular document, such as the *Magna Carta*, remains the same, whether it is printed on paper, or vellum, or silk, or merely recited aloud. Indeed we sometimes say that two documents, even though their wording may be rather different, are "substantially" the same – if in effect they both mean the same thing. Or yet again, we may say, "Don't read the whole document, just give me the substance of it." This second use of the word "substance" refers to the essential nature of the thing we are talking about, quite apart from the material form in which it happens to be presented to us. So, in the Creed, this word "substance" must not be taken to mean that either God the Father or God the Son is composed of any kind of stuff or material. "Of one substance" means that they share one and the same essential nature. In other words, the Son is not just "rather like God"; He <u>is</u>, in the very essence of His nature, God Himself.

That being so, how are we expected to distinguish God the Son from God the Father?

Last week we made a picture of this; we saw that we could make a distinction, without supposing any essential difference, between the word and the thought. The Creed offers another "picture", it calls the Son "Light of Light", and St Augustine develops this a little further. He says that the Son is to the Father "as the ray is to the light".[5] Again, in another picture phrase he explains that the Son is to the Father "as the jet of the fountain is to the water".[6] These two pictures may suggest something to us. The ray derives from the light, it is "begotten" of the light – yet we cannot separate it from the light – it is the light. Nor can we separate the jet from the water – it is the water. What, then, is special about the ray and the jet which distinguish them, without separating them, from the light and the water?

The distinction, wouldn't you say, is this: that the ray and the jet of the fountain are light and water in their activity – going somewhere, doing something, displaying energy, forming themselves into a pattern; just as the word is thought in activity communicating itself to others. So all these three picture-phrases suggest that God the Son is God in his activity – making things, expressing himself, manifesting himself. They are both God – they are both the same God, and yet they are really and truly distinct: just as when I am writing a book, the book which I have in my mind is the same book which I write down on paper – exactly the same in substance, although it is quite easy to distinguish one from the other, and to realise them as having each an individual manner of existing. The book in my head is really there, though you cannot see it and can only believe in it by faith; the book I write is the same book actively expressing itself in words, and creating a material form that you can see and recognise.

With this idea in our minds, let us turn back to the Creed and see if there is

---

5 Unfortunately, Sayers' memory was at fault here. The passage in question comes from Lactantius's *Divine Institutes* 4:28-29, written around A.D. 307.
"When we speak of God the Father and God the Son, we do not speak of them as different, nor do we separate them, because the Father cannot exist without the Son, nor can the Son be separated from the Father, since the name of 'Father' cannot be given without the Son, nor can the Son be begotten without the Father. ... [T]hey both have one mind, one spirit, one substance; but the former [the Father] is as it were an overflowing fountain, the latter [the Son] as a stream flowing forth from it. The former as the sun, the latter as it were a ray [of light] extended from the sun." Sayers had realised her error by the time she wrote *The Emperor Constantine*. Lactantius is a character in the play, and Sayers puts his words into the mouth of Athanasius at the Council of Nicaea.
6 This is probably a reference to St Augustine's *Treatise on Faith & the Creed (De Fide et Symbolo)*, chapter 9.
"For take the instance of an interrogation on the subject of a fountain, and consider how we are unable then to affirm that the said fountain is itself the river; and how, when we are asked about the river, we are as little able to call it the fountain; and, again, how we are equally unable to designate the draught, which comes of the fountain or the river, either river or fountain. Nevertheless, in the case of this trinity we use the name water [for the whole]; and when the question is put regarding each of these separately, we reply in each several instance that the thing is water."

anything there to confirm that we are thinking along the right lines. Yes, there is. The conclusion to which all this description of God the Son leads up shows us precisely the Son in His activity. It is He "by whom all things were made". (This is clearer in the original than in the English translation. The words aren't meant to read "of one substance with the-Father-by-whom-all-things-were-made", though they may sound like that when read carelessly or quickly. There is a semi-colon after "Father" and a fresh start; it is the <u>Son</u> who is of the Father's substance, and the Son again by whom all things were made.)

The Son, then, is the active power in the creation of the world. The Father creates by, or through, the Son. The Father is the Thought, the Son is the Word begotten of that thought; both equally create that great Book of the Universe which is unrolled in the scroll of time. When we come next Sunday to talk about the part which God the Son played in human history, it is very important to remember this. There is not one God who made the world and another who came to live in it; it was the actual creator Himself, very God of very God, who lived hard and died horribly in the world that He had himself created.

3. The Man of Men

Forces: Sunday 22nd June 1941: 2.50 - 3.00 pm (Recorded)

"One Lord Jesus Christ ... who for us men and for our salvation came down from Heaven. And was incarnate by the Holy Ghost of the Virgin Mary. And was made Man."

On these last two Sundays we have been examining what the Creed has to say about God the Son – God our Lord, the Divine Energy who made the world, and who is of one nature with God the Father, yet distinct from Him as the word and the thought are one and yet distinct. Today, we begin to deal with the clauses which tell us that this same God and Lord is actually the same person as the village carpenter called Jesus of Nazareth; so that when we speak to God we can call Him, not merely "Lord", but "Lord Jesus".

This part of the Creed tells the story of God's great adventure – how for one brief interval in history, God – the maker of time and space and matter – became one of his own creatures, subject to the natural laws of time, space and matter, and living as a man among men.

At the outset, we come up against a rather difficult phrase about Man. The Creed says that this adventure was undertaken by God "for us men and for our salvation". Salvation. In order to save us. From what? The shortest answer that can be made is: "from our own sinful selves".

You will notice that the Creed does not enter into any explanations about sin; it accepts human sinfulness as an obvious fact, something which anyone can recognise in himself without further argument. And, indeed, thoughtful men have always felt that there was something queer about man – something that makes him at the same time much better and much worse than a plant or an animal. He alone is consciously and intentionally good; he alone is consciously and wilfully bad. And when he is bad, he knows all the time that he doesn't really want to be like that. There is, as modern psychologists recognise, a kind of inner dislocation in his will, which makes him desire one thing and do another. This is the condition which theologians call "sin" or "sinfulness". Man's will is free to choose good or evil; but he suffers under some kind of inhibition, so that he is not really free to do, in his own strength, the good he chooses. He is like an invaded country. Some kind of inner weakness or treachery has put him under the yoke of a hateful tyranny, and his only hope is in a counter-invasion by a more powerful force of good, with which he can cooperate to regain the free possession of his own soul.[7]

The Christian doctrine is that not only can the power of God enter into each individual soul and so help men to overcome their individual sinfulness, but also that God did once actually invade history, so that the whole course of world events might be redeemed and turned to good by His tremendous energy. "For us men and for our salvation", God became a character in history, and so made the meaning of history plain to us. He showed by His example how evil could be redeemed, and he also brought into history the power by which that victory could be accomplished.

So, at a time and place in history, God the Son "came down from Heaven". This does not, of course, mean that He ceased to be God, or left His place in Heaven empty. When he entered our world of space-time-matter in the form of a man, He no more departed from Heaven than the words which we speak depart from our mind when we utter them or write them and so give them a material form. "Heaven" is not a place, but what is called a mode of existence; at Bethlehem, God entered upon a new mode of existence. Words can very well be active in two "modes of existence" at once: in the "mode" of thought and in the "mode" of the printed page. And so the well-known hymn speaks of God the Son: "the heavenly word proceeding forth, yet leaving not the Father's side".[8]

In this sense, therefore, God "came down from Heaven" and "was incarnate" – that is, He entered upon an existence in the mode of flesh and blood; He became a part of the animal world, governed by the laws of animal biology. And, "He was made Man" – He became a human person, with a mind as well as a body, and subject to all the ordinary human limitations of mind and body.

---

[7] Sayers may well have taken this image from John Donne's Holy Sonnet XIV:
"I, like an usurp'd town, to another due,
Labour to admit you, but O, to no end.
Reason, your viceroy in me, me should defend,
But is captived, and proves weak or untrue.
Yet dearly I love you, and would be loved fain,
But am betroth'd unto your enemy;
Divorce me, untie, or break that knot again,
Take me to you, imprison me, for I,
Except you enthrall me, never shall be free,
Nor ever chaste, except you ravish me."

[8] These are the first two lines of J. M. Neale's translation of Thomas Aquinas's Latin hymn *Verbum supernum prodiens*. Sayers probably knew it as Hymn 311 in *Hymns Ancient & Modern*.

To all, this is, except one. He was without sin. He had a human will – so that we can say, in a sense, that He was free to sin if he liked; but it would be more true to say that He, alone among men, was free not to sin. There was no inner dislocation of His will, because His personality was God's personality and His will perfectly one with the will of God, who wills nothing but good. I think it is worthwhile just to stress that point. When the theologians say that Jesus was "without sin", they do not mean that there was a mechanical impediment that made Him incapable of sin, as a hedgehog is incapable of hopping like a kangaroo. They mean something more like what we mean when we say: "So-and-so is incapable of such an action – it is not in his character."

Thus, considered as a human person, Jesus is the pattern of what Man might be if Man had never known sin. He is "perfect man" in two senses. He is really and altogether man – not a mixed monster like a merman or a sort of apparition with the outward shape of a man and no more; but a genuine human being with the thoughts and feelings proper to every man. And He is man in a state of perfection, with a single will turned undeviatingly to the goodness that is God. But, being born into a sinful world, He could not escape the consequences of human sin. Those He had to bear, as the innocent must always bear the sin of the guilty, just because He was truly man, and all men are members one of another. We know how, when a nation becomes false to itself and commits dishonourable actions, the people who feel the shame of that guilt most acutely, and are readiest to redeem it by their own suffering, are those loyal men who took no part in the betrayal. They feel the sins of their countrymen as their own, because of the bond of blood between them.[9] So the sinless manhood of God experienced all the pain and all the horror of the sinful humanity He shared – a horror all the greater because there was nothing in His will that could for one moment assent to sin. Thus St Paul, in a bold image, says that God "was made sin for us, though He knew no sin."[10]

You will notice that I have left out two phrases: He was incarnate "by the Holy Ghost of the Virgin Mary". The full doctrine of the Holy Ghost – the Third Person of the blessed Trinity – will be dealt with later on in this series.

---

[9] Sayers may well have been thinking of the French resistance to Pétain and the Vichy régime as she had recently read the testimony of Elie J. Bois, which she later quoted in "The Other Six Deadly Sins". Bois himself, the former editor of Le Petit Parisien, corresponds entirely to the description. She could equally well, however, be referring to the Confessing Church in Germany.

[10] 2 Corinthians 5:21.

For the moment, we must just note that it means "by the living power of God", and leave it at that.

With the expression "of the Virgin Mary", we touch upon the question of miracle. This, too, I will leave for the moment, because time is short, and it will be easier to deal with the whole subject of miracles when we come to the Resurrection.

But one thing it is important to emphasise here. The incarnate God did not enter the world altogether from the outside. He was born in the world, as a part of the creation, the son of a human mother. His conception was not just a spiritual revelation; it was also a physical fact. Unlike all the idealist philosophies and spiritual cults, Christianity is of the earth, earthy, solidly clamped to the material body of the visible creation and bound up with the human nature we know. The Tree of Life lifts up its flowers and fruit to the splendour of the Light Invisible; but its roots are fast in the soil of earthly history, and the record of its planting is furnished with a human name and a date.

4. The Death of God

Forces: Sunday 29th June 1941: 2.50 - 3.00 pm (Recorded)

"And was crucified also for us, under Pontius Pilate: He suffered, and was buried."

Last Sunday we spoke of the birth of Jesus, the perfect Man who was at the same time perfect God. Today we are to speak of His Death.

Yes; but haven't we missed out something? How about His life? What has become of His teaching, His behaviour, His miracles and works of mercy, His prophecies, His "message", – and above all, of that elaborate edifice of Christian morals on which we are accustomed to lay such stress, as though they were the only things that really mattered about the Man called Jesus? Surely a Christian Creed should have something to say about them?

The Creed says nothing whatever. Not a word. Not a syllable. It lays all the emphasis, not upon what Jesus said, but upon what He was. And, indeed, the people who exhort us to "follow the teaching of Jesus", regardless of whether such a person ever actually existed, and whether He was God or not, are putting the cart before the horse. If He was not true God, and true Man, His words and works are of no more importance than the words and works of Marcus Aurelius or Karl Marx or the heathen oracles. It is only when we believe in Jesus that is becomes urgently necessary to believe Him. The axis on which the Christian faith revolves is the belief that God once passed through the world in living flesh and blood; and on that belief the Creed concentrates, to the exclusion of all other considerations.

Very well, then. God, says the Creed, came into the world in the nature of a perfect Man. The world saw perfect goodness, perfect innocence, perfect justice, perfect mercy, perfect beauty – with its own eyes it saw God. Having seen Him, it promptly decided that God was a dangerous criminal, and handed Him over to the common hangman.

Of all the indictments ever made against human society, that is the most fearful. It is so appalling, if we really think about it, that men have twisted it this way and that way, and invented all kinds of ingenious explanations to avoid admitting the truth of that ghastly accusation. Only the other day, a minister of religion thrust away as intolerable the idea that God was hanged on the gallows of the cross: "It was an idea," he said, "to shock all reverent minds". It is, indeed – and in the name of reverence, various heresies have been put forward to relieve mankind of that burden of intolerable guilt. There were the heresies of the Gnostics, asserting either that Jesus had no real human nature, and therefore could not really suffer, or that the Divine nature was withdrawn from Him before the crucifixion, so that what suffered and died was not God, but only the shell of His humanity. And there were – and still are – the Arian heretics,[11] who said that Jesus was indeed a man with an exceptional likeness to God and a more than ordinary share of the divine nature, but not true God in nature and person. Against these heresies, and the innumerable variations of them, stands up the Catholic Church, affirming in the teeth of the world that that which died upon the cross was true God and true man – that every agony that man can undergo – grief, pain, fear, shame and defeat and death, passed through the consciousness of God and are for ever part of God's experience. That there was even one terrible moment when God experienced the final depth of human wretchedness – the utter degradation of sin and the sense of being forgotten and abandoned by God; and that when he uttered that desolate cry "My God, my God, why hast Thou forsaken Me?"[12] God felt the shadow of the horror that is called despair, and knew what it was to be divided from Himself.

That is the staggering claim which Christianity makes. And when we consider it, we may see why the Church laid such emphasis upon those words: "God the Son, of one substance with the Father", and was ready to defend them with her life. For they stood for two truths of vital importance: first, that it was God, the world's Creator, who had thus known and suffered all that man could know or suffer in the world – God Himself – not some helpless victim, different from God, and vaguely known as His Son – but God of God, Light of Light, Very God of Very God, by whom all things were made. And secondly, that all the evil suffered by God in time and space is known to His Divine Self, not as evil, but as good. It is known to Him for ever in Heaven – not as a bitter memory of past pain, but as a perpetual triumph, because he is one with the everlasting Father, in Whom there is neither evil, nor toil, nor pain, nor passion, but only the perpetual joy of all goodness.

God suffered and God died: that is the godward side of the crucifixion.

---

[11] Followers of the theologian Arius (c. AD 250-336), who taught that God the Father and the Son did not exist together eternally. Arius also taught that the pre-incarnate Jesus was a divine being created by (and possibly inferior to) God the Father. Sayers included him as a character in her play *The Emperor Constantine*.

[12] Matthew 27:46

But there is also the manward side. Because Jesus was truly man, it is possible for all men, through His experience, to know pain and suffering and evil as He knows them – as good, and not as evil. When God passed through the grave and gate of death, He took all human nature with Him. Short of destroying humanity, God could not abolish human sin and evil; but by passing through the universe, He could redeem evil – that is, He could make it good – for himself and for all mankind.

Now: the thing to remember about this staggering story is this: the Church asserts that it really happened. Legends of martyred gods are common enough – Mithra, Osiris, Adonis – there are a hundred such. But their lives and deaths are placed in some dim period outside human history. The story of Jesus is quite a different tale. "He was crucified under Pontius Pilate." Why should this Roman governor be specifically mentioned in the Creed? He was not exceptionally wicked. He was not the person chiefly responsible. The people chiefly responsible were the priests of the Jewish Church, who resented as a dangerous blasphemy the claim that Jesus was the Son of God, and who feared and hated the living Energy which came to shatter and transform their formal interpretations of the moral law. Because of their fear and hatred, they represented to Pilate that Jesus was setting Himself up as an earthly king, the leader of a religious and national revival that would raise up the kingdom of Judaea in rebellion against the Roman Empire. Pilate was an ordinary Roman official, rather in the position of the Governor of a Crown Colony, – a man of no great imagination or strength of character, certainly, but quite without personal animus against Jesus. He was doing his duty, as he saw it, to the State which he represented, taking the line of least resistance in putting down a movement which seemed to him to have dangerous political possibilities. Why, then, should the name of this unfortunate and not very important man be handed down, century after century, repeated day by day in the Creed, in connection with the world's worst crime, rather than the names of the malevolent High Priest Caiaphas or Judas who betrayed his master?

Pilate is mentioned, not as an object of special execration, but because his name fixes the date. The god Osiris was slain nobody knows when – there is no attempt to pin his legend to human history. But the God Jesus was "crucified under Pontius Pilate". Flatly, definitely, in the same matter-of-fact way that we might say "Jack Sheppard was hanged in George I's reign"[13], the Creed

---

[13] Jack Sheppard was a notorious housebreaker and thief in early 18th century London. Renowned for his spectacular escapes from Newgate prison, he was finally hanged in 1724 at the age of 23. The character of Macheath in John Gay's *Beggar's Opera* is said to be based on Sheppard.

asserts that God was executed in the reign of Tiberius Caesar – not "once upon a time" like the gods of myth and legend, but in one of the most prosaic, well-documented and intellectually "advanced" periods of human history, a time full of military operations, social legislation, politics, education, hygiene and theatrical entertainments. Jesus was not just symbolically "Man", He was not only "the perfect Man"; He was a particular man; He was a character in history, and God from everlasting to everlasting.

5. The World's Desire

Forces: Sunday 6th July 1941: 2.50 - 3.00 pm
(Recorded in London on Tuesday 24th June 1941)

"And the third day He rose again, according to the Scriptures, and ascended into heaven; and sitteth on the right hand of the Father."

On Friday, the Man who was God died on the public gallows. The body was examined by the officials responsible for the execution, pronounced to be quite dead, and buried in a sealed tomb. On the Sunday morning, the tomb was found open; the body was gone and the Man was seen alive.

This, we say, is a miracle. If it is true, we can accept all other miracles without distinction – virgin birth, healing the sick, multiplying the loaves and fishes, quelling the storm. There is only one principle in question. Can the thing we call soul, mind, spirit, will, which we cannot see or touch, but of which we seem to have intimate personal experience – can this invisible thing really control that other kind of thing which we see and feel, and to which we give the name of matter, or can it not?

Now, there is nothing in itself abnormal, or even unusual, in seeing matter pushed and pulled about, and generally controlled, by invisible and intangible forces. That is precisely the way in which our own bodies seem to be controlled. We do not call it a miracle when some twelve solid stone or so of our own flesh and blood gets up out of a chair and walks across the room at the bidding of our will and fancy; it seems to us quite natural and ordinary. But we should call it a miracle if, by merely willing it, we could move mountains about; because we assume the mountain to be something quite apart from ourselves – separate and different.

This assumption was quite reasonable in the days when matter was thought to be divided up into distinct categories which had nothing much in common, and when mind and matter were supposed to be two totally different things. But today, the scientists[14] who have analysed matter most closely assure us that

---

[14] Although Dorothy L. Sayers had no formal scientific training, she tried to keep up-to-date with the latest trends in science and the philosophy of science. The wartime reading list published at the end of *Begin Here* in January 1940 included two studies of contemporary scientific thought: A. N. Whitehead's *Science & the Modern World* (Lowell lectures 1925) and John Macmurray's recently

between one kind of matter and another there is practically no difference, except a difference of atomic arrangement – a difference of form. And moreover, that the further they carry their analysis, the more difficult it becomes to define any essential distinction between matter and mind. They are not all agreed whether to call mind a form of matter, or to call matter a form of mind: but they do agree that throughout the universe – men, animals, plants, rocks, air, electricity, space itself – they cannot find anywhere any break in the continuity of this stuff. Everything is part of the one great tissue of moving atoms – spread more thickly here and more thinly there, moving faster in one place and more slowly in another, but nowhere discontinuous. We and the mountain are arranged very differently, to be sure; but we are linked together by that matter which (according to some modern physicists) bears a very strong appearance of being the same stuff of which our minds are made.

Here is a third point: nowhere in the story of Jesus is it claimed for Him that <u>because He was God</u> he had a special and unique capacity for working miracles. On the contrary, He himself said that anybody could work miracles – provided he had faith; provided, that is, he could empty his will of self-will, and so leave it open for the power of God to use. If the miracle-worker became self-absorbed – like St Peter when he tried to walk on the water and got frightened[15] – or if he were surrounded by a hostile atmosphere of selfishness and unbelief (as sometimes happened to Jesus himself) then no miracle was possible.[16] But the power of God which made and moves the whole material universe was available to any and every man, given the right conditions.

Lastly, we said a few Sundays ago that Jesus was not only perfect God, but perfect Man – He is Man as man ought to be and would be, if he had not fallen into the sin of self-absorption.

The suggestion we get from these four points is this: that so-called miraculous power over the material universe is not a thing abnormal to men. It is a power which man should and would possess by nature, were it not for the sinful and divided will that, on the one hand, cuts him off from the power of God and, on

---

published best-seller *The Boundaries of Science* (1939). Various quotations in *The Mind of the Maker*, which was published just as this series of talks was being broadcast, showed that Sayers had recently read Sir Arthur Eddington's *Nature of the Physical World* (1927) and *The Philosophy of Physical Science* (1938), Sir James Jeans' *Eos* (1928) and Reginald Kapp's *Science versus Materialism* (1940).

[15] See Matthew 14:22-33.
[16] See Matthew 13:57-58.

the other, makes him imagine a discontinuity – a barrier – which is not really there between himself and other material beings. So that in Jesus, the perfect Man, we see man restored to his <u>normal relations</u> with God and nature, moving and acting as freely within the whole material universe as he does within his own material body.

But now comes an important question: if such is, or ought to be, the nature of a normal man, living an earthly life, what happens after death? Does he lose touch with matter and form altogether? Or does he remain master of the creative will and power that manifests itself continually in fresh material forms?

Now let us look at the accounts given to us of the Resurrection of Jesus – particularly at the account in the Gospel according to St John, which is the only one that claims to be an eye-witness report. When the disciples came to the empty tomb, they saw the long linen bandages which had been swathed round the body lying there, and the handkerchief which had been wrapped around the head – not tumbled upon the linen bandages, as though thrown there by somebody getting up and unwrapping himself, but placed at a little distance, and still in its original folds.[17] The picture we get is as though the dead matter of the body had been resolved into its very elements, drawn right out through the wrappings without disturbing them, and reassembled elsewhere in a new form.

And it was, indeed, quite a new form of matter that showed itself to the disciples after the resurrection. In some ways it was like the body of the living Jesus, but in others it was very different. Though it could be seen and heard and handled, though it could walk and eat and drink, it was curiously fluid and unstable. It could pass through closed doors, it appeared and disappeared unaccountably, and it was not always immediately recognisable. It was as though it was held together by the direct power of a perfectly free and perfectly authoritative will, that could shape and unshape matter as it chose – as though the disciples were witnessing the creative mind actually at work to fashion itself a form out of – we might say – any atomic material that happened to be handy. For forty days it demonstrated its free control over the matter that had once conditioned it; then, having done all it came to do, the Heavenly Word departed from the material world, and returned to the eternal Mind in that Heaven from which it had never been absent.

Thus, says the Creed, the God who was Man rose from the dead "according

---

17   John 20:7.

to the Scriptures" – as the Scriptures had foretold that He would. That, said the risen Jesus, when he talked to the disciples at Emmaus, was what the Jewish prophets had been driving at, when they talked of the Christ of God who was to come. And not the Jewish prophecies alone. All the religions of the world, whose prophets had dreamed of a God – Mithra, Osiris, Adonis – who should be made Man, and die, and rise again, found their fulfilment in Jesus Christ. Men had always felt that somehow God must be like that, and (says the Church) they were perfectly right. God and Man died on the Cross; God and Man rose from the dead – rose in creative power, the master and not the servant of material form, and "sat down at the right hand of the Father" – God and Man inseparably united in that single, undivided Person who fulfilled the world's desire.

6. The Touchstone of History

Forces: Sunday 13th July 1941: 2.50 - 3.00 pm (Recorded)

"And he shall come again in glory to judge both the quick and the dead; whose kingdom shall have no end."

The words "divine judgement" are often used in a very thoughtless and un-Christian sense. People used to be fond of saying that some disaster, such as a disease or accident, was "a judgement" upon the victim for sins which had nothing to do with causing the disaster – as though God were a kind of crusty old magistrate, imposing an arbitrary scale of penalties for the infringement of a moral code. It is often supposed that that is what the Christian means by "divine judgement", though Christ Himself said very plainly that this idea was entirely mistaken. God's judgements are always the consequences, direct or indirect, of an offence against the universal law: if you hold your hand in the fire, you will be burned; if you swallow prussic acid you will die; if you are wicked and greedy enough to exhaust your soil by over-cropping, the whole country will become a rainless and sandy desert, swept by whirlwinds and barren of food. This kind of judgement may take a long time and involve many people besides the offender, because men are so closely bound up together that we can take no action without affecting others, and because (as we saw last Sunday) we are inextricably linked by nature with the whole material universe. Nor can such judgements be remitted or altered; they can only be redeemed by toil and sacrifice and the willing acceptance of consequences – as, for example, when men and governments devote money and labour to reclaiming an area which greed and idleness have devastated. God allows the nature of things to fulfil itself in all its consequences; He does not concern Himself with the administration of penal codes. "Man", said Jesus, when He was asked to arbitrate in the matter of a legacy, "who made me a judge, or a divider over you?"[18] And He added, "Beware of covetousness" – thus removing the whole question from the sphere of earthly legality to a sphere of grace in which the law of equity is not abrogated, but fulfilled by becoming an expression of free generosity. Now we have seen that God the Son is the "sole-begotten" of the Father – God's word is consistent and does not contradict itself, whether in heaven or on earth. Therefore, when the Creed speaks of God the Son "coming to judge all men, dead or alive", we shall expect this "last judgement" to be of the same kind as all His other judgements.

---

[18] Luke 12:14.

Now the words of Jesus, and the whole of the New Testament, are full of strange prophecies of that "last day" in which the heavenly Judge shall appear in power and glory to establish the eternal values of all men and their works. The prophecies are of course expressed, as all prophecies must be, in metaphors – picture language – drawn from the world of our experience: angels, clouds, trumpets, the breaking-up of graves, the gathering of God's people from the ends of the earth, and so on. And it is hard to discover from the Gospels exactly how or when all this is supposed to be going to happen. Sometimes Jesus seems to speak as though the event was following closely on the times in which He lived, and many of the early Christians thought the world would not outlast the first century. Sometimes He spoke as though it would not happen for a very long time; and sometimes He said He did not know when it would happen – only the Father knew that. There has been a great deal of argument about it; some people, taking the metaphors literally, have made elaborate calculations about the exact date of the end of the world; others have said that Christ, having only a human intellect, shared the general ignorance and superstitions of His day about time and space and matter; yet others have argued that He cannot have been God, because if He had been, he would have known all about it and supplied a handy calendar for mankind to work to.

But this kind of argument is quite meaningless: because, though the language used about judgement <u>has</u> to be our kind of language, using metaphors drawn from time and space, the judgement itself has really nothing to do with time and space. "The last day" means precisely "the last day" – it will destroy time. It is of the nature of eternity, within which all time, past, present, and to come, is included and lost. It is thus known only to the Father, who is timeless. It is not easy to think of existence without time; modern physicists may announce its arrival, and expound it terms of the Fourth Dimension and the Second Law of Thermodynamics, but their scientific explanations do not enable us to imagine it, and are chiefly helpful to theology as a warning against taking any kind of picture-phrases too literally.

But there are three things we are, I think, safe in saying about the judgement. First, that it will be of the divine kind – not arbitrary, but the necessary consequences of men's conduct and belief. Secondly, the value of everything men do and are in this world of time and space will be judged – that is, will exhibit itself – in relation to those eternal values which are God, and which were made known to men in the person and teaching of Christ the Word, who is the very being of God acting in time and space.

And thirdly: it is the incarnate Word that will judge the world. When Jesus speaks of his return in judgement, he calls Himself not "Son of God" but by the old Jewish title for the Messiah and Redeemer of Israel – "Ye shall see the Son of Man coming".[19] Man (to use again the picture language of the earthly law courts) will be judged by no alien standards; he will be judged, in the old jury phrase, by his peer – by the One who made Himself Man's equal, and who knows all the facts about man by experience and from the inside. He is judged by what man should be, could be, and was – by the perfect human nature that was taken up into an eternal union with the divine nature of God. Jesus, God and Man, is the touchstone of history, and His judgement reveals the meaning of all history in an eternal present for which the words "beginning" and "end" have no meaning.

So we come to the end of that part of the Creed which deals with God the Son. You will have noticed that it is closely packed with technical terms, part of whose meaning I have tried to explain. Theology is called "the divine science" and like other sciences it has compressed the results of its investigations into technical formulae. People sometimes say, "give us pure religion, we don't want Creeds". This is rather like saying, "give us pure arithmetic; we don't want the multiplication table". The Creed is a formula embodying man's experience of God, as the multiplication table is a formula embodying man's experience of the mysterious and invisible thing we call number. The multiplication table does not become irrelevant to experience merely because it is sometimes gabbled thoughtlessly by children. To everyone there comes from time to time the moment when "twice two is four" ceases to be a parrot-chant about pure number and acquires an urgent personal significance in eggs or onions or pounds, shillings and pence.

And so with the Creeds. We may recite them for many years without troubling to think what the words really mean: and call ourselves Christians without defining to ourselves exactly who or what Christ was; but when we are really challenged as to why we should believe His teaching or look to Him to rebuild the crazy structure of human civilisation, we shall find it of vital importance to whether we believe Him to be just one teacher among others, or in the words of the Creed: "Very God of very God, by whom all things were made: incarnate, crucified, dead and risen; the judge, whose kingdom shall have no end."

---

[19] Matthew 24:30.

71

Christ & the Radio Padre[1]

11th February, 1943

The Rev. Dr. J. W. Welch,
Box No. 7,
G.P.O.,
BEDFORD.

Dear James,

I have just received the current Christian News-Letter, containing the "Mass-Observation"[2] report on religion. The thing that strikes me most forcibly is that, judging by that report, nobody would suppose – if he didn't know already – that the "religion" in question was Christianity. It is true that one reply quoted starts with "Christianity says –" followed by a quotation from the Sermon on the Mount. Apart from that, the only religion people seem to have ever heard about from the Churches is a little mild theism (as preached, no doubt, by an itinerant teacher in Galilee). But where is the faith of "Jesus Christ and Him crucified" to everybody totally unaware that Christianity is "about" the death of God and the redemption of the world by the suffering of the innocent? It looks as though, for anything that the Churches have been able to drive into the head of the public, Christ might just as well never have been crucified at all. That's what I mean when I say that they've got the most terrific story in the world, and they don't tell it. They talk a dickens of a lot about Christian principles and love and kindness and moral behaviour and social reform – every blessed thing about the Christian *Hamlet* except the Prince of Denmark. Is there any other subject in the world about which so much is said, with any apparent attempt to ensure that the listener knows what the thing is all about? Whether he then believes it or does anything in consequence is a different matter – but he ought surely to be told what it is.

I was listening to your radio padre[3] last night, talking about faith in God.

---

[1]   Wade Center File 448/40-42.
[2]   A social research organisation founded in 1937, which aimed at recording all aspects of everyday life in Britain.
[3]   Rev. Ronald Selby Wright (1908-1995), Minister of the Church of Scotland.

Well, that was all right. But when his interlocutor asked whether it was necessary to believe the Creeds and all that, he waved the Creeds aside, said it wasn't necessary to remain in the shallows worrying about details – one should go for the deep things and have faith in <u>God</u>. Since nobody, up to that point, had mentioned Christ <u>at all</u>, I could only conclude that He was one of the superfluous details to be swept up with the rest of the rubbish, and was really quite surprised to hear Him mentioned afterwards in a parenthesis and in I forget what context – I think it was something about Him having "shown God to us".

I admire the Archbishops[4] for their gallant attempt to cope with the social and economic situation; but really, if it's <u>Christianity</u> they are concerned about, the best thing they could do would be to instruct their clergy that for the next twelve months, Sundays and week-days, in season and out of season, they should preach God incarnate and Christ crucified – a thing for which there is plenty of apostolic precedent – and leave the Sermon on the Mount and the reformation of banking and even kindness to animals until they had made people aware that Christianity was about <u>Christ</u>: not primarily about what He said about behaviour, but WHO He was and What He DID.

I wish some of your BBC statisticians would look through the scripts of religious broadcasts over a stated period and see what proportion of them deal a) with Christ at all (otherwise than as a teacher of ethics) and b) with the Cross (and under this I don't count pathetic allusions to "our dear Lord who loved us so much and died for us" unless there is some attempt to relate that death to the central Christian position; otherwise one might just as well work up emotion about the death of Socrates or the death of Nelson). And I don't count as really properly "dealing with Christ" the casual dragging in of his name as an afterthought, like the perfunctory "through Jesus Christ our Lord" mumbled at the end of a prayer apparently addressed to somebody quite different – which, for all it conveys to the heathen and the uninstructed, might almost be "per Carter Paterson",[5] or "by favour of Mrs Jones", or "by kind permission of the Columbia Broadcasting Company."

Of course I'm being very sweeping and unjust. But if I could have hit that

---

[4] William Temple (Archbishop of Canterbury), Cyril Garbett (Archbishop of York) and possibly also Arthur Cardinal Hinsley (Roman Catholic Archbishop of Westminster).

[5] Carter Paterson & Co. Ltd were carriers and delivery agents. Sayers used them for transporting costumes and scenery for her plays.

padre last night with a brick, I would have thrown it. The C.N.L. this morning confirmed me in the impression that "religion" as the common man gets hold of it is no more centred in Christ than Geometry is centred in Euclid – they are just people who happen to teach a subject rather well, that's all.

The whole thing's so unfair. If you were God, and had taken the trouble to go through all that humiliation and suffering to redeem the world, wouldn't you be a bit hurt in your feelings to find that, two thousand years after, people were still saying they didn't think there could be a God, or he wouldn't allow nasty things to happen, and your own bishops (yes, bishops!) were bleating that they couldn't understand why God in His inscrutable providence allowed the suffering of the innocent? Great heavens! If they don't understand by this time, they ought to. Christians are the only people who have no atom of excuse for not understanding. What on earth have they been about? – I know what they have been about. They have been saying: "Be virtuous and you will prosper", like the Old Testament Jews, instead of saying like Christians, "Be good and you will be crucified; the innocent always pay, because they are the only people who have anything to give – that's what it means to be part of the mystical body of God, who was good and paid the price. So far as you are bad, of course, you are suffering the consequence of badness, and leaving others to redeem it, but just so far as you are good, you are helping God to pay for you and for everybody else." There's plenty left in that to argue about and explain – but how anybody calling himself Christian can have the face to say he doesn't know why the suffering of the innocent is allowed or what it's for, beats me. I tell you, James, they've never read the story. They can't have. Of course, they may think it an untrue story or an immoral story. If they do, they should stop pretending to be Christians and be something else. But they've no right to suppress the story or tell a different story altogether.

I nearly wrote all this to the C.N.L., I but I can express myself more pungently to you: besides, I'd be interested in those statistics!

Tell Eric Fenn, I don't think I can manage those dialogues. The domestic situation is still bad (though I'm hoping for an improvement), the Archbishop of Canterbury is clamouring about the "H.C.F. of Consent",[6] I still haven't done a play for Val, I am plunged in correspondence, encouraging a man to write a book for *Bridgeheads* about the profit motive, and I'm still fretting

---

[6] See Giles WATSON, "The Oecumenical Penguin", *SEVEN*, vol.14, 1997, p.7-32.

about Darlan.[7] And *Agape* is not my subject. If things get easier later on, I'll let you know.

Yours ever,

Dorothy

---

[7] Dorothy Sayers started to write a radio play about Admiral Darlan but never completed it. See Christopher DEAN, "Admiral Darlan", *Studies in Sayers: Essays presented to Dr Barbara Reynolds on her Eightieth Birthday*, The Dorothy L. Sayers Society, 1994.

"The Gospel is a thing of terror" [8]

Stephen Grenfell Esq.[9]
The BBC,
200 Oxford Street,
LONDON W1.

Dear Mr Grenfell,

I did receive your letter, but as it was long and I was very busy, I laid it aside, as you requested, for "a more convenient season".

However, I have now read it.

I sympathize very much with all your feelings, but I feel sure that, if I am to be any help to you or to your generation, it cannot be by just meeting and talking. I am a writer, and if I have anything to contribute to what is, rather oddly, called the "post-war world", the best way I can do it is by writing, and not by entering directly into schemes for "planning" and so forth. If you have read the first chapter or two of Stephen Spender's *Life and the Poet*,[10] you will see the kind of thing that is likely to happen when the writer strays out of his job and tries to deal with world-affairs in a medium which is not his own.

You found something you wanted in *The Man Born to Be King*.[11] I am glad of that, because the writing of plays is my proper job. There, it seems, I have succeeded to some extent in "getting across" with something. And that is the way I have to do it – by writing. Anything else is likely to be make-shift and second-best.

---

[8] Wade Center File 411/17-24.
[9] Stephen Grenfell, a young employee of the BBC, wrote a 7-page letter to Dorothy L. Sayers on 22-23 May 1943 expressing his appreciation of *The Man Born To Be King* and explaining what he perceived to be the religious questions and problems of his generation.
[10] Stephen SPENDER, *Life & the Poet*, Secker & Warburg, 1942.
[11] Grenfell had not heard the plays, but read them in the version published by Victor Gollancz in May 1943.

But I think I should like to put down something about what you call the "story of Jesus Christ". As I have told it, as the Church has always told it, as Catholic Christianity has always believed it, it is not the story of "a young man named Jesus" – it is a story about <u>God</u>. I think the thing that contributed perhaps most of all to the chaos and misery of your generation, and indeed of my own, was that they had forgotten that it was a story about God. They could not understand why earthly hopes should turn out to be illusory, human ideals issue (in practice) in hideous travesties of themselves, "progress" turn round and go backwards, the old brutality burst up under the crust of civilisation, and chaos appear to have come again. It was not only that they suffered – they were dumbfounded, and the bottom of their universe had fallen out. The only people who were not, and could not be, <u>astonished</u> were those who remembered what the story of Christ was about. It is the story of how man killed and murdered God; and it is the epitome of all history. Christians know quite well that innocence goes to the cross, for what was crucified was innocence itself. They know that there is no trust to be placed in "human progress" as such, nor in any child of man;[12] and that increased scientific knowledge can only widen the scope and power both of good and evil, not alter their essential antagonism. The battle is never over. There is no "security" in this world, nor ever can be – no final security. The story of Jesus is not a story of intolerance towards a progressive young man, which a little education and kindness of heart would have amended – it is God who is on the cross.

I entirely agree that the problem after the War will be the problem of the war-weary. The danger was, is, and will be, that we shall again imagine that at the end of physical warfare we ought to be able to sink reposefully into a condition of stability or "normality", requiring no further conflict. That is what we tried to do last time. We were trying to do the impossible. What happened was that we lapsed into a state of mental torpor and neutrality, under cover of which the old conflicts went on in a different mode. We said that it was just that people had "different ideas" – ideas didn't matter – all truth was relative – good and evil were just names for different points of view – until the conflict burst out, like fire that has been damped down, and incarnated itself in a physical and bloody shape which we could not ignore.

All living is a desperate adventure, and there is <u>no</u> point at which we can

---

12 An allusion to Psalm 146:3, "Put not your trust in princes nor in any child of man, for there is no help in them."

sit back and say "the war is over". There has to be "eternal vigilance".[13] The thing that the Christian Church forgot to teach people these last few centuries, or was howled down and called a nasty old sour-puss[14] if she <u>did</u> teach it, was that every human soul carries within it that seed of corruption and that will to death which is technically called "original sin", and that this corruption is manifest, not simply in our vices, <u>but also in our virtues and our ideals</u>. (You need not quarrel with the <u>word</u> "sin" – psychologists know it under a different name, and even those who loudly deny it as a doctrine recognise it as a <u>fact</u> of existence.) Because of it, everything we do has a sort of inner kink in it which makes it defeat itself if it is allowed its own way. Rescue a man from poverty, and he will promptly lose the virtues of the poor and develop the peculiar vices of the well-to-do; rescue the serf from slavery to the soil; you will find that what you have given him is the instability of the factory worker; destroy nationalism, and you are faced with the rootless internationalism of finance; take away the readiness to war, and you produce a state of mind that acquiesces in <u>any</u> cruelty and <u>any</u> treachery, rather than take up arms to oppose it; take off all restraints from sexual passion, and you find that the passion is lost, and you are left with a dull and jaded promiscuity; abolish illiteracy, and you hand the people over to the intellectual delights of the *Daily Mirror* and the propagandist – and so on and on for ever. Yet, you cannot merely let things alone, for if you do they will merely become worse and worse. You are perpetually walking along a razor-edge of peril – "a fire on the one hand and a deep water on the other"; perpetually building up what is always falling down.

The trouble with the "Debunking Period" was that it "debunked" everything that could be shown to have developed a flaw, without considering that it is the nature of everything that man does to develop flaws and vices. The people imagined (for their philosophers had told them so) that man had only to discover some formula or other and carry it out to reach the Golden Age. When the formula did not work, they thought there must be sabotage somewhere, and savagely turned to smash whatever suitable fetish seemed to present itself – politicians, capitalists,

---

[13] "The condition upon which God hath given liberty to man is *eternal vigilance*; and which condition if he break; servitude is at once the consequence of his crime and the punishment of his guilt." John Philpot Curran, *Speech upon the Right of Election*, 1790. The quotation: "The price of freedom is eternal vigilance", is also frequently attributed to Andrew Jackson and Thomas Jefferson.

[14] Sayers herself received an anonymous postcard which began "You nasty old sour-puss" after the final broadcast of the series *The Man Born To Be King*. See Barbara REYNOLDS (ed.), *The Letters of Dorothy L. Sayers vol.2: from novelist to playwright*, The Dorothy L. Sayers Society, 1997, p.375.

Jews, Bolshevists, churches, Colonel Blimp [15] – anybody who could be made into a whipping boy. But the trouble is in man himself, as they would have known if they had not discarded the old theology in favour of the new humanism.

Listen, you say that the youth of the world is casting about blindly, "seeking something which it does not understand." It is "on the move," but it doesn't know where it's going. Now, Christianity cannot perhaps tell you which road you will take; the one thing it can tell you is where you are going, and that is to the place where all roads lead. You are going to Calvary. Everything that is of God in you is going to be crucified; and everything in you that is of corruption is going there to crucify the good part. To whatever Kingdom of God you are going in this world or the next, you must go by Calvary Hill. Did you notice what I made Our Lady say in *King of Sorrows*? –

> From the beginning of the world until now, this is the only thing that has ever really happened. When you have understood that, you will understand all prophecies and all history.[16]

And so long as you do understand it, it is all right. You will be going with God and knowing what you are doing and where you are going. But if you continue to think that there is some way round, so as to cut out Calvary, you will not find it, and you will be disillusioned all over again. You will still come to Calvary with God, but you will be Gestas and not Dysmas,[17] and will die swearing and sneering at God instead of going into Paradise with Him. Man's vices – the Caiaphas, Pilate and Judas in him – don't merely crucify the virtues they detest; they crucify their fellow-vices as well; and the vices die screaming and debunking everything, and their death brings no redemption.

In war, you know, the drama that is always going on is brought down on to the physical plane and everybody can see what it is. In war the facts are stripped naked, and (generally speaking) we accept them for what they are. That is war's great and terrible virtue. In that crude and violent and concrete form we <u>see</u> why no victory can be won without blood and toil, tears and sweat, and the suffering of thousands of innocent people. It is all painted on such a gigantic

---

[15] Reactionary, jingoistic cartoon character invented by David Low in the 1930s.

[16] *The Man Born To Be King*, p.295.

[17] Dorothy Sayers describes Gestas, the unrepentant thief as a "plain brute, foul-mouthed... vindictive" (p.290). Her Dysmas, the other thief, who speaks kindly to Christ, is still human and open enough to be able to recognise something of who He is and can therefore find salvation.

scale and in such glaring colours that we can't miss it. But we have got it into our heads that peace is different. It isn't. It's exactly the same. War is not an interruption to life; it is life. Peace demands exactly the same energies, the same virtues, the same crucifixions, only translated into different terms. If once you see that, you will accept it as people accept the facts of war. Because the story of Jesus is not just the story of one event, or of a few especially atrocious events – it is the pattern of all history and there is no other.

It is, I think, a deprivation to be brought up only on *The Descent of Man*[18] and *The Martyrdom of Man*;[19] and never to have been told the Christian story – the Fall of Man, and the Martyrdom of God.

In great things and small, it is all the same story: the men who fell before Dunkirk without the weapons that could have saved them were bearing in their bodies the sins of the whole world – the neglects and the egotism and the self-seeking of the rulers and voters and citizens (including themselves, for no man is ever wholly innocent) who let that situation come about; whether they knew it or not, they died as God died for the sin and folly of those to whom they were bound in the unity of the flesh. In so far as they themselves were guilty, their death was judgement; but in so far as they were innocent, their deaths were like the death of God – pure gift of themselves to redeem those sins. The children killed in a bombing raid die like the Holy Innocents – guiltless and unknowing – their deaths pure gift to the world that the Christ-Child may be saved to walk with open eyes to the cross. The weariness of waiting in queues, the stuffiness of the black-out, the irritation of saving fuel and paper, are little hourly crucifixions by which the innocent redeem the waste and destruction of the guilty. We take each others' sins – Hitler's, the Government's, the Church's, yours and mine – everybody's – up into our own lives, and by great or small acts of suffering make the damage good. The victims of peace suffer and die no otherwise. It is the pattern of the life of God.

When you thought of God as a "powerful administrator, who ......"[20] and so on – were you thinking of Him nailed hand and foot to the cross of man's

---

[18] Charles DARWIN, *The Descent of Man* (1871) – Darwin applies his theories outlined in *The Origin of Species* to human evolution.

[19] Winwood READE, *The Martyrdom of Man* (1872) – a poetic, freethinking and evolutionary history of the world.

[20] Stephen Grenfell had referred God as "a powerful enough administrator but one, who because he was at the head of a job too de-centralized for one mind, has made rather a mess of things". (Wade Center, File 411/27.)

brutality? Probably not. But that's where He is, you know. That's where we put Him. But all you saw on the cross was the progressive young man with internationalist politics in advance of His time. My dear boy, if God had walked this world three thousand years later than He did, internationalists would have killed Him just as surely as the Jewish nationalists and the Roman imperialists. More surely, perhaps. International organisations tend to ruthlessness: neither international finance nor international communism is especially notable for tenderness in its methods, and if we start a system of "international police" it is likely to deal summarily with people who don't toe the line.

I cannot tell you what is going to happen in the "post-war world" – (do you see why I said that was an odd phrase? It draws a line of separation which is not really there) – nor even, very specifically, what it ought to aim for. I can only tell you that unless it begins by understanding what sort of creature man is, and what sort of story we are living through, it has no hope of accomplishing anything. And if it demands that Christianity should show it a short-cut to an easy Utopia, it is asking the impossible. It is true that Christianity today is not in a healthy state – its prophets, too many of them, prophesied falsely and the people loved to have it so. They wanted a nice Father-Christmas sort of God, who would let the children "express themselves", and do as they liked – and when that was duly preached to them they spat it out for pap, which it was. They would not look at the terrible Lord of Glory nailed on the gibbet of history. They thought man was all right – man was the master of things – till they suddenly met man face to face at Passchendale,[21] or at Dunkirk, or in the concentration camps, or in the squalor of betrayal and avarice and cruelty and filth and dishonesty. Then they cried aloud to the Father-Christmas-God who was the only God they had ever heard of. But God was not in the nursery, handing out presents to good boys – He was on the cross beside them.

"Jesus", said Pascal, "is in agony until the end of the world."[22] "For the whole creation," said St Paul, "groaneth and travaileth together, filling up that which is lacking of the sufferings of Christ".[23] The Church of Christ is His

---

[21] Popular name for the 3rd Battle of Ypres, a particularly horrific battle during World War I, which took place between July and November 1917. There were about 310,000 British casualties.

[22] Blaise PASCAL, *The Mystery of Jesus,* 553.

[23] Sayers appears to have combined two well-known Bible verses: Romans 8:22, "For we know that the whole creation groaneth and travaileth in pain together until now" and Colossians 1:24, "Now I rejoice in my sufferings for your sake, and in my flesh I complete what is lacking in Christ's afflictions for the sake of his body, that is, the Church."

mystical body, in which He suffers throughout time. She knows (or should know) what she is doing and why. The whole creation is in another sense His mystical body, in which He suffers; but those outside the Church do not understand what they are doing or why – their suffering is inexplicable to them and borne without will, without joy and without hope. The Church's suffering is (or ought to be, if Christians were able to act up to their beliefs) borne willingly, in joy and in hope, because she knows herself to be suffering in, with, and for God. As one great Christian put it: "If any man will carry his cross, the cross shall carry him".[24] – I say that it should be so, I do not say it always is so: the Church, too, is made up of sinful men.

I don't know what they told you in your childhood or boyhood about Christ. But if they told you that He was only a man with "ideas about" religion and ethics and brotherhood and internationalism and the working man, and all that, then what they told you had nothing to do with Christianity. Nothing at all. It was just another human story. Even as a human story, it was a lie, for the Jesus of the Gospels was not like that at all. He was a person who gave laws in His own name as though He were God, who demanded the kind of allegiance due only to God, who said that he would judge all men in the last day, who forgave sins in His own right, who asserted that He and God were one, who said "the man who has seen me has seen God",[25] and who proclaimed that He would be seen "sitting at the right hand of power and coming in the clouds of Heaven".[26] Virtuous young men with ideas do not talk like that. "He was", as C. S. Lewis says, "either a raving lunatic of an unusually abominable type, or else He was, and is, precisely what He said".[27] You cannot cut and carve the Gospels and the tradition so as to extract from them a human Jesus with no claims to Godhead. People have tried to do it, and in the end found they had carved away everything, and there was no Jesus left. You cannot have a merely human Jesus with no supernatural claims – there is no evidence that such a person ever existed. But there is plenty of evidence of a Jesus with supernatural claims, and you can take your choice about that: you can say He was a liar, you can say He was a lunatic, or you can say with the Church,

---

[24] Probably a reference to Thomas à Kempis, *The Imitation of Christ*, chapter 37: "If you bear the cross willingly, it will bear you and lead you to your desired goal, where pain shall be no more; but it will not be in this life."
[25] This is probably a reference to John 14:9, "Anyone who has seen me has seen the Father."
[26] Matthew 26:64, "Jesus said to him, 'You have said so. But I tell you, hereafter you will see the Son of man seated at the right hand of Power, and coming on the clouds of heaven.'"
[27] C.S. LEWIS, *The Problem of Pain*, Geoffrey Bles, 1940, p.11-12.

"God of God, Light of Light, Very God of Very God, by whom all things were made, who was incarnate and made man".[28] But if you say what the Church says, then you have to revise your ideas about God and about man. You have got to choose between crucifying God and being crucified with Him: no other choice is open to you or me or any man. When you have understood this, you will understand all prophecies and all history. Then you can set out to make a Christian world, knowing what you are making. But not till then.

You may very likely think the Church is wrong about Jesus Christ. Very well. Then He was a liar or a lunatic: leave Him out of it. Build a pagan world, dedicated to Man. But if you do, and if the Church is right after all, God will still be crucified in that world, and you will be there, shouting with the crowd, or hammering in the nails, or washing your hands, or pocketing the thirty pieces,[29] or rending your garments in the most high-minded and respectable manner.[30] And you will all be extremely astonished to find that your attempts to achieve security and the Kingdom on earth will end, as before, in fire and sword and the tramp of the legionaries through the inner court of the Temple. You will be astonished, because you will have acted all through from the best possible motives, like the Crowd and the soldiers, and the Pharisees and Caiaphas and Pilate and probably even Judas. They "did not know what they were doing",[31] because they had got the wrong idea about God. They thought He was sitting somewhere above them, patting them on the head; but He was there among them, being crucified.

That is the Christian story. It is scarcely an incantation; I do not know that it is a threat exactly; but it is not soothing syrup. "The Gospel is a thing of terror"; it is Good News to those who suffer, but it is not good news to those who look for security.

Nothing in the speeches of post-war planners terrifies me so much as the word "security". I am not, in practice, a very good Christian, but to anybody – even the weakest and worst sort of person – whoever has once seen the Christian pattern of the universe and grasped, however feebly, what it means, nothing can ever look the same again. The clatter of the people who have

---

[28] Extracts from the Nicene Creed.
[29] Judas Iscariot's thirty pieces of silver.
[30] Allusion to Matthew 26:65, "Then the high priest rent his garments, saying, 'He has spoken blasphemy: what further need have we of witnesses'?"
[31] Allusion to Luke 23:34, "Jesus said, 'Father, forgive them, for they do not know what they are doing.'"

apparently never glimpsed that meaning, even as a possibility, is frightening. In the last war, my husband saw some Chinese coolies, cheerfully building a cooking-oven out of live ammunition; and it's rather like that. A lot of busyness and doing things, without the slightest understanding of the nature of the stuff they are handling.

You say that *The Man Born to Be King* afforded you a "cool, satisfying, though fleeting, caravanserai." If so, that is the measure of its failure. God is not just in the caravanserai – though He is there for those who have found Him; He is in the desert, walking to His death.

Yours very sincerely,

Dorothy L. Sayers

The Devil and the Coffee Pot[32]

11th November, 1943

The Rev. Dr. J. W. Welch,
The BBC,
Box No. 7,
G.P.O.,
BEDFORD.

Dear James,

This morning, after reading your letter, I was getting my breakfast when I had a sudden illumination! It must have been genuine, because the Devil, seeing it come into my mind, was so angry that he overthrew the coffee-pot (which was standing all by itself on the stove, doing no harm to anybody) and poured a pint and a half of freshly-made coffee over the gas-grill and the floor and into a small pan of fish-cakes which I was in the act of frying. However, he got nothing by it except a little bad language.

This was it:–

The moment the Devil sees that somebody may be really going to preach the Gospel, he puts it into their heads to announce that a Challenge has been issued to the Churches. Instantly everyone's attention is diverted from the Gospel and focused on the Challenger, the Churches, the Preachers, the BBC ... Christendom, organised Religion, the Need for a More Spiritual Outlook, the Social Crisis, or anything else that usefully pushes God into the background.

Blow (if I may put it that way) the challenge to your preaching at the microphone! Whatever you do, don't suggest publically that you have been challenged. Everybody is only too anxious to rush in and criticise and agree that the whole trouble with Christianity is bad preaching. Nothing will delight the Devil more than to see them all chasing after this beautiful stuffed electric hare. The minute you say you have been challenged, *you* step into the centre of the picture and everybody dismisses God from their minds to take a good, satisfying look at Broadcasting House.

---

[32] Wade Center File 448/6-11.

When they hiked Paul into the Areopagus and asked him to explain himself, he didn't say: "Men of Athens! A most important challenge has been issued to my preaching –" He just said, "Look here – you're all in a muddle, worshipping you don't know what. I am now going to tell you about God."[33] And told them the story.

Never mind the challenging letters from clever listeners. It will only fix people's minds on the writer of the letter ("so striking") and on you answering it ("so courageous"). After all, you and I and the Radio Padre and the Archbishops and Uncle Tom Cobley and all are of the utmost insignificance. You don't want listeners to look at a dogfight – you want them to look at Christ. Tell them who God is, and what He does and did. Tell them God was crucified, and that they have got to be crucified too. (Because that's what they want to know – they want to know that their suffering makes sense. And it's no good saying they can't understand it, they've got to understand it – that's what it's all about. And a few of them will understand it, even if it's only Dionysius the Areopagite and a woman named Damaris[34].) Keep on telling them. Make them keep their eye on the ball, and not look round to see what you and I and the Church are doing. Challenges to the Churches don't matter a hoot – we have one every six months and nothing comes of it but a few headlines in the daily press. The important thing is the mutual challenge between God and Man, and we don't want to turn it into a triangular duel.

Just go and preach the Gospel at the Market Cross.[35] Never mind the wigs and gloves on the green – the Devil only throws them there to divert people's attention. He doesn't mind what they look at so long as it isn't the Cross.

I'm sorry I'm being obstructive again. But this is the message the Devil was so anxious you shouldn't receive. (He gave himself away by his stupid manoeuvre with the coffee-pot.)

---

[33] Paraphrase of Acts 17:22-23, "Paul then stood up in the meeting of the Areopagus and said: 'Men of Athens! I see that in every way you are very religious. For as I walked around and looked carefully at your objects of worship, I even found an altar with this inscription: TO AN UNKNOWN GOD. Now what you worship as something unknown I am going to proclaim to you.'"

[34] Allusion to Acts 17:34, "However, certain people joined him, and believed: among whom were Dionysius the Areopagite, and a woman named Damaris, and others with them."

[35] The usual place of public preaching for the early Protestant preachers in Britain. John Bunyan, for example, preached at the Market Cross in Bedford.

Yours ever,

Dorothy L. S

P.S. 1   Of course, if you feel you've been challenged, it's all right to tell one another and tell the Bishops so. But don't tell the people about it. <u>Tell them the STORY</u>.

P.S. 2   (Friday morning) – Your roneo script just arrived. Here are one of two points which occur to me:–

1.   I think the point that gets obscured is quite simply the Divinity of Christ. If you really believe that Jesus is GOD (though in the morphé of a servant and the nature of a man) then "to think of God and men as Jesus does" means something more than and different from the face-value of the words – it means you've got to think with God's mind (not so easy!).

2.   "How does it work out in a parish?" "What difference does it make to washing-day?" Well, that's the point. Why does <u>crucified God</u> make more difference to washing-day than Socrates drinking hemlock? If it doesn't, why call yourselves Christians? Christianity was called the Way. But Jesus said: "<u>I am</u> the Way." [36] – not I'll show you the way. I suppose that on washing-day the Christian washerwoman is, so to speak, "carrying" the general dirtiness of the world. In the same sort of way, when we have to do without a fire on a cold night to save fuel, we (comparatively innocent) are to that extent "carrying" the stupidity of ministers (political ministers, I mean, not parsons!), the tiresomeness and lack of charity between miners and owners, and the guilt of war which makes extra coal necessary. By our willing acceptance of that "little daily crucifixion" the deficit is wiped out and the evil sterilised. It <u>finishes</u> there… We <u>take</u> the other people's guilt and carry it, and so redeem it and there's an end. If we refuse, then the evil continues to propagate itself, – armies are destroyed and battles lost for lack of coal. Or if we violently resent the sacrifice, we start a fresh cycle of anger and hatred and trouble. As a matter of fact, <u>in an emergency</u>

---

[36] John 14:6, "Jesus answered, 'I am the way and the truth and the life. No one comes to the Father except through me.'"

when we are strongly conscious of our solidarity with ministers and miners, however sinful, because they and we are one in blood, we do feel that the act of atonement is not only expedient, but right – for a brief moment we really see the pattern of the Cross as the pattern of life. God, being Incarnate, therefore solid in blood and nature with Man can "carry the guilt" of mankind because He is at once perfect Innocence and perfect Charity (which we can never be); it is the Incarnation which at one and the same time confirms the validity of the pattern and gives the power to live the pattern; as Eric Fenn says, you've got to make this clear.

3.   It is interesting that Cyril Taylor "never heard the Bishop of Bristol[37] speak of the Cross." One could scarcely imagine a bigger break with the Apostles: "Christ Jesus and Him crucified,"[38] "this Jesus whom ye crucified, made both Lord and Christ,"[39] "God forbid that I should glory save in the Cross,"[40] and all the rest of it.

4.   It is true that people don't think of themselves nowadays as "miserable sinners."[41] But they are desperately aware that something is frightfully wrong with the world. Sometimes,…. They say they think "man must be a kind of disease in the world". Sometimes they feel that they are in the power of uncontrollable, impersonal, and malignant demons (all sorts, ranging from 'Economics' to 'the unconscious'), so that all their efforts are useless. Or they externalise the wrongness and load it on to convenient whipping-boys, Jews, Capitalists, Hitler, and so on, and try to expel the irritant by persecution and destruction. They play their personal lives as light comedy because they simply daren't face the universal tragedy.

5.   It may be that in a sense, I am "overcalling my hand" – but Eric Fenn must remember that in one of those two letters I was making a specific

---

[37]   The Rt Rev. Clifford Woodward.

[38]   St Paul in 1 Corinthians 2:22, "For I resolved to know nothing while I was with you except Christ Jesus and him crucified."

[39]   Acts 2:36, "Therefore let all the house of Israel know assuredly, that God hath made the same Jesus, whom ye have crucified, both Lord and Christ."

[40]   Galatians 6:14, "But God forbid that I should glory, save in the cross of our Lord Jesus Christ…"

[41]   The Litany in the *Book of Common Prayer* has the refrain: "O God the Father of heaven: have mercy upon us miserable sinners." The General Confession also says: "But thou, O Lord, have mercy upon us miserable offenders."

criticism, and in the other I was dealing with a specific complaint by a very angry and miserable young man.[42] I could say quite a lot of other, quite different, things about the consequences of the Incarnation – e.g. the "freeing of the images", and the enormously important results to secular Art and the secular State. But they wouldn't have been relevant in the circumstances. The questions that people chiefly ask at the moment are two: a) Why does everything we do go wrong and pile itself up into some 'monstrous consummation'? and b) What is the meaning of all this suffering? The Christian answer to the first is, "Sin," and to the second, "Christ crucified."

Or isn't it? I have always supposed it was, and the Saints and Apostles seem to have thought so. But nowadays it seems to be just a matter of 'facing problems in the spirit of Jesus' or 'thinking like Jesus' or 'adopting the attitude of Jesus'. And supposing you do these things, what is likely to happen to you? Why, since human nature doesn't change very much, somebody will crucify you, to be sure. And what good does that do? Everything, if the Crucified is God; you are living the pattern of the universe. But if He is not God – well, evil has had another victory and that is all. The Bishop of Southwark's[43] summary (quoted by Cyril Taylor) is full of those curious ambiguities to which we have grown accustomed: "The life and spirit of Christ" – does he mean the earthly example and the "attitude", or does he mean the indwelling life upholding all the creation, and the Holy Ghost? "The good news of God about Himself" – does he mean that Jesus gave us some information about God, or that He revealed Himself as God in action? "At once truly divine and truly human" – does he mean "Very God of Very God",[44] or does he mean "displaying that heavenly nature of which there is a spark in all men"?[45] "To face life's problems, sin, suffering etc. in his spirit" – spirit again! – "in the light of his forgiveness, sympathy, courage, endurance" – does he mean the thing we call the Remission of Sins or just a general "spirit of amiability"? And there isn't a word about Redemption of Sin – either by Christ or (after our fashion) by us. "To think of God and men as Jesus does" – Well! – "to share in the power and wisdom of that life" – does he mean Almighty Power, the Wisdom of the *Logos*, and the Life of the Eternally Begotten, or does he mean the influence of the earthly

---

[42] Mr L. T. Duff.
[43] The Rt Rev. Bertram Fitzgerald Simpson.
[44] Quotation from the Nicene Creed.
[45] A point of view shared by Gnosticism and, more recently, by Transcendentalists like Emerson, Theosophists or liberal clergy at the beginning of the 20th century, who were influenced by evolutionary thought.

life of a great and good man? – "The fact that this is possible" – What makes it possible? – All these words can be interpreted in two ways, and have an air of being deliberately chosen to avoid coming down on either side of the fence.

That is not what I mean by "telling the story". It's shying away from the story. I quite agree that (for the "outsider") you have to get rid of the technical term and the evangelical language. By all means interpret the story in terms of washing-day and coal-shortage and unemployment and bombs. By "the story of Christ" I don't mean the story of the exemplary young carpenter. I mean the story of the act of God in the world.

You don't really need two thousand words of challenging letter. Five will do: What think ye of Christ? [46]

Note: the "monstrous consummation" – Eric Fenn is dead right about this – the seeds of decay and death in movements for social reform – sin corrupts the whole of man's nature, including his virtues – the emergence of the enantiodrome [47] when any human value has been endowed with absolute value (i.e. deified).

There's another point: that the corruption begins as it were inside and at the top (it is the fall of a spirit) and tends to work down and out, as it were, incarnating itself in lower coarser forms: first, a spiritual rebellion; next, an intellectual conflict; lastly, a crude and violent physical struggle. As a rule we don't notice the first stage, approve of the second in the name of liberty of opinion, and are astonished and horrified by the third, which appears to us quite inexplicable as well as abominable. The fact is we don't pay much attention to evil until it affects the body.

---

[46] Christ's question to the Pharisees in Matthew 22:42, but also the title of many sermons by famous preachers, including George Whitefield, J. C. Ryle, Charles Raven and Dwight Moody.

[47] An enantiodrome, or contranym, is a word which has two or more distinct and contradictory meanings.

The Nature of Redemption[48]

20th November, 1943

The Rev. Dr. J. W. Welch,
The BBC,
Box No. 7,
G.P.O.,
BEDFORD.

Dear James,

Right-oh! Let's make it December 6th, then. That fits in best with my domestic arrangements, which at present are so ordered and settled (though not upon the best and surest foundation) as to give a little more liberty at the beginning of the week than heretofore.

About the *Kerygma*[49] – a fine, chunky and learned sounding word for it, I haven't much more to say really; it is only one or two points in other people's letters I had sort of skimmed over without proper attention.

The point made by both Taylor and Fenn is that the "story" of Crucified God appears irrelevant because people nowadays have no sense of sin. That, of course, is literally the *crux*. It is impossible to preach the Cross without preaching sin. Reinhold Niebuhr in *Nature & Destiny of Man* (Vol I, Ch. 4)[50] has a long section about the "Easy Conscience of Modern Man". I'm a very poor person to appreciate modern man's feelings on all this, because I can't think of any personal misfortunes which have befallen me which were not, in one way or another, my own fault. I don't mean this necessarily in the profounder and more religious sense. I mean that I know jolly well that if anything unpleasant has happened to me in life I had usually "asked for it". Consequently, when I talk about carrying the sins of the world, I'm going outside my experience – anything I have to put up with looks to the life like the direct punishment of

---

48 Wade Center File 448/2-5.

49 The *Kergyma* is the element of proclamation in Christian apologetics, as contrasted with the *Didache*, or teaching element. It is often used as shorthand for the basic Gospel message.

50 This was the published version of Niebuhr's Gifford Lectures, given at the University of Edinburgh in 1940.

my own sins, and not leave much margin over for redeeming other people's. But I do see that most people today look upon themselves as the victims of undeserved misfortunes, which they (as individuals & as a species) have done nothing to provoke. Contemporary literature and thought seem to be steeped in self-pity, which is the most enervating state of mind imaginable.

If only they could start from the idea that there is "something funny about man" – and that he does tend to fight against the right order of things, they could get a more robust outlook on suffering and catastrophe, and see that they were carrying:

a)   the direct consequences of their own wrongness – the "punitive" element in suffering

b)   the indirect consequences of other people's wrongness – the "redemptive" element (this concerns, of course, chiefly what Taylor calls "our cross rather than Christ's; but I can't see how God's cross can be seen to be relevant before the sinful nature of Man and the nature of "redemption" is understood. "Redemption" really meant something to a nation that knew slavery).

One big stumbling block in the way of all this is the extraordinary reluctance of modern man to accept the idea that an action must have consequences. He doesn't see why he should ever have to take a step from which there is no retreat. There's a flight from the *libertas minor*[51] – a flight from real choice. I remember Alan Wheatley[52] saying: "I can't bear all this killing – it's so irrevocable." All Death is irrevocable – that's why we find it such an outrage. But we feel that everything else ought to be revocable, modifiable. Nobody will allow that something could really happen, which divides BC from AD, and as a result of which the world can never be the same again. That would mean committing one's self to something; and we feel we ought always to be able to revise decisions and prevent them from having consequences... Now, that point of view I quite understand, in the sense that I detest committing myself – but my brain tells me it's quite unreasonable. Verbally, I think Fenn gives in a little to this way of thinking when he talks about 'a fresh start' and 'escape from

---

[51]   "The lesser freedom" – Augustine of Hippo used the term to refer to freedom of choice or freedom within the law, as opposed to the *libertas major*, which was the freedom beyond the law to make the right choices to serve God and the common good.

[52]   Radio announcer and actor. He played Judas Iscariot in the original broadcasts of *The Man Born To Be King*.

the meshes of our past chains and past mistakes'. There isn't, of course, any 'escape' or 'fresh start' in the sense of <u>abolishing</u> the past and its consequences. The past can never be wiped out, but only redeemed and 'made good': (that, I am sure, is what he really means – it's only his words that mislead a little). To <u>escape</u> from the past would be Christ's coming down from the Cross; to redeem the past means going through the Cross to the Resurrection. One muddle about forgiveness is of the same kind – forgiveness is the restoration of a good relationship, but it doesn't abolish the consequence of the offence, nor is it going back to where we were before the offence was committed. It's got to be a new relationship (in that sense, certainly, a 'fresh start') which contains and transmutes the disturbance caused by the offence. If I borrow money from you and squander it, your forgiving the debt doesn't put back the money – that's lost and you bear the loss and so "carry the guilt". If I get in a rage with you and throw your best teapot out of a window, no amount of forgiveness will unbreak the teapot – all we can aim for is a relationship in which both you and <u>I</u> can bear to sit down and breakfast together out of a shaving mug without feeling uncomfortable and without an ostentatious avoidance of the subject of teapots. The universe can't "break the iron law of cause and effect" – that would mean an irrational universe; but the effects can be so "made good" that the whole process is redeemed – "*O felix culpa –*".[53]

The flying buttresses in Salisbury Cathedral are the most beautiful thing in the world – but they came out of a fault in the building. The central tower was built up higher than the original arches could carry & a great spire put on, & the walls began to bulge outwards. On the exterior, a later architect added the flying buttresses & redeemed the fault by making the thing lovelier than it would have been if the fault had never been committed. (He didn't, as a matter of fact, redeem it wholly, because the strain was still too great & the pressure on the tower arches was subsequently relieved from inside by a set of cross arches which are a botch and an abiding horror; the architect at Wells found a better way of redemption with those curious inverted arches which are really rather beautiful.) So far as the outside goes, anyway, Salisbury is the better for its buttresses, though anybody who knows anything can see they are the redemption of an evil past – "carrying the guilt" of whoever it was that wanted a more ostentatious spire than his foundation could afford. The law of cause and effect isn't broken, but the error is redeemed, & the final result is <u>better</u>.

---

[53] "O fortunate crime!" – Phrase taken from the Exsultet hymn in the liturgy for Holy Saturday.

I think it's here that the relevancy of the Cross comes in – that the Power which made and sustains the universe, with its iron laws, is the Power that (not prevents evil from happening, which would make freedom of choice unmeaning, but) makes evil good. As Taylor says: if the *didache* had been <u>everything</u> – if it was only a question of saying, "Behave like this & evil won't occur," Christ might as well have gone back into Heaven & never been crucified at all. That, we may imagine, is the sort of thing that could have happened if there had never been a Fall – i.e. God could have just shown Himself & explained the working of the Law, & departed. But since sinfulness had happened & couldn't unhappen, He had to show Himself as that which makes evil good in & through the working of the Law of Sin.

(I can't think I'm expressing this at all clearly; but I'm struggling with Niebuhr, who is, I am sure, most important, but very difficult, & quite exhausting to the brain.)

By the way, our old friend & enemy, "scientific method" is largely responsible for the unwillingness to commit one's self to a decision, because it fosters the notion that all theories are tentative & liable to revision. Therefore people brought up on the idea that scientific method is all the method there is & can't bear to admit a "final revelation", or a happening that can't be unhappened, or a choice made without reservation. Naturally, since acts & events do in fact happen and can't be unhappened, they are always finding their experience in contradiction to their ideology, which gives them the feeling that something oppressive is being done to them from outside, & they're being "put upon" by the universe. Hence they dislike history, & are always trying to escape into the future – which they hope will (somehow or other) start afresh with a clean sheet. And they are always attempting to make the past unhappen by reinterpreting its events so as to show that no decision was ever really decisive. Like the man in Eliot's *The Family Reunion*, they find the return into history

> "Painful, because everything is irrevocable,
> Because the past is irremediable,
> Because the future can only be built
> Upon the real past."[54]

He tells his family – no, he tells the girl as a matter of fact –

---

[54] T. S. Eliot, *The Family Reunion*, Part I, scene I (Faber & Faber, 1939).

"One thing you cannot know;
The sudden extinction of every alternative,
The unexpected crash of the iron cataract".[55]

That's the thing everybody fears & pretends doesn't & can't happen –

"First of all, you isolate the single event
As something so dreadful that it couldn't have happened,
Because you could not bear it. So you must believe
That I suffer from delusions – "[56]

Eliot's got his finger on something in that play – & golly! How everybody hates it, including the critics! It would be grand on the wireless, but I suppose everybody would hate it again.

Anyhow, when you tell people that there's a dead-line drawn between BC & AD they have to believe that you 'suffer from delusions'".

Isn't it odd that the first Apostles quoted the <u>words</u> of Christ so little, & we quote them so much? We always think we're addressing people who know the story – they knew they weren't.

Oh, well!

Yours ever,

Dorothy L. Sayers

---

[55] *The Family Reunion,* Part I, scene II.
[56] *The Family Reunion,* Part I, scene I.

Thought for the Day[1]

A correspondent the other day in *The Daily Telegraph* was complaining (very rightly for all I know) of the "lugubrious tone & depressing counsels" of the gentleman who broadcasts the "Thought for the Day" at 7.55 am.[2] His letter, written shortly after the evacuation of Dunkirk, contains some interesting assumptions about the nature of faith. (Incidentally, a most illuminating survey of the effects of religious instruction could be compiled from letters to the papers; it is here that the average man lets himself go on the subject of faith & morals, & reveals, not only what he has been taught, but what he has understood from the teaching.) The following passage deserves analysis, & would indeed provide the text for a nice little course of sermons:–

> When, moreover, he [the broadcaster] keeps insisting that our present troubles are due to our lack of faith & sinfulness, he becomes as exasperating to listen to as he is patently illogical. The nation hardly needs to be reproved for lukewarm faith when it has just offered a thanksgiving for what it believes to have been miraculously answered prayers.

We will pass over the candid and manly avowal that it is exasperating to be told we are sinners & that that we do not in fact consider ourselves to be any such thing. Three discourses at least would be needed to deal with it: one on the Fall, one on pride and the third on the unpopularity of prophecy. We will examine only the argument about faith. The writer's line of thought is perfectly clear, & is undoubtedly based upon Scripture. It invokes the authority of logic, & takes the form of a syllogism:–

What we ask faithfully, we shall obtain effectually.[3]
We obtained effectually;
Therefore we asked faithfully.

If the logician should object that we have here an undistributed middle,[4] the

---

[1]   Wade Center File, Sotheby's Lot 293 iii.

[2]   At this period the actual programme was called *Lift up your Hearts: A Thought for To-day*. The speakers for this programme changed regularly. It was unusual for any one person to do more than seven days in a row. James Welch and Eric Fenn were responsible for the choice of contributors and often spoke themselves.

[3]   Quotation from the "Collect for the Twenty-Third Sunday after Trinity" in *The Book of Common Prayer*.

[4]   A syllogistic fallacy, for example: All penguins are black and white, all old films are black and white – therefore a penguin is an old film.

writer may reply by citing Matt. XIII.58[5] & XVII.20[6], restating his syllogism accordingly:

Where there is no belief, there is no miracle;
but there was a miracle;
therefore there was belief.

To this logic one can scarcely object, unless by disputing the minor premise;[7] a thing which divinity would scarcely wish to do, though it might seize the opportunity for a fourth sermon, on the Nature of Miracle. Divinity might, however, point out that God's mercies are seldom strictly proportional to the quantity or quality of the petitioner's faith. The removal of mountains is no proof of a mountainous degree of faith, but at most of faith "as a grain of mustard-seed"; are we content to leave our faith in this seedy condition? On the lowest grounds we should encourage it to grow, hoping that if a seed will move mountains a whole tree might lever up the world. Better still, it should be encouraged for the sheer beauty of its natural growth. There is something sordid in that kind of heavenly bookkeeping which shows a payment of a quid of miracle against a quo of faith; & it is very doubtful whether the Lord of the Vineyard balances his books on that principle. I am reminded of another indignant letter in another paper, discussing the case of a lame man who had made the pilgrimage to Lourdes & not been healed. "The man," said this correspondent, "had a right to expect a miracle." God had, so to speak, taken his money on false pretences. This would provide matter for a fifth sermon – On the Origin & Nature of Rights – & I do not envy the preacher. If he is honest he will make himself very unpopular.

The sixth sermon for which our quotation supplies a text will bear the title: On Religious Sentimentality. This, I fancy, is really at the bottom of this confession about faith and answers to prayer.

There is a kind of story very much beloved of film-audiences & readers of serial fiction. It is all about a man who has a love-affair with a glamour-girl. But his love – his _real_ love – is given all the time to his wife. He does not

---

[5] "And he did not many mighty works there because of their unbelief."
[6] "And Jesus said unto them, Because of your unbelief: for verily I say unto you, If ye have faith as a grain of mustard seed, ye shall say unto this mountain, Remove hence to yonder place; and it shall remove; and nothing shall be impossible unto you."
[7] A specific statement in a syllogism which may or may not follow on from the major premise or generalisation.

express it in any way, but it is all the more real for that. We know it is real, because when the glamour-girl deserts him & financial troubles thicken (?)[8] about him, it is to his wife that he turns. "There was never <u>really</u>", he assures her, "anybody but you." He has, in fact, been <u>really</u> faithful to her all along. In return, he feels confident that she will see him through. She does.

---

[8] This word is illegible in the original manuscript apart from the 'th" at the beginning.